"COME BACK TOMORROW"

African Memories

David Costello, OCD

"Come Back Tomorrow": African Memories

Published by Wheatmark®
2030 East Speedway Boulevard, Suite 106
Tucson, Arizona 85719 USA
www.wheatmark.com

ISBN: 978-1-62787-919-4 (paperback)
ISBN: 978-1-62787-920-0 (ebook)
LCCN: 2021919113

Bulk ordering discounts are available through Wheatmark, Inc. For more information, email orders@wheatmark.com or call 1-888-934-0888.

Property of the Discalced Carmelite Province of Calif.-Az.
All proceeds from the sale of this book go toward the support of the Carmelite Mission in Uganda.

Scripture texts used in this book are taken from the New American Bible. The Old Testament of the New American Bible copyright 1970, by the Confraterenity of Christian Doctrine (CCD). Washington, DC. Revised New Testament of the New American Bible copyright 1986 CCD. Revised Psalms of the New American Bible Copyright 1991 CCD.

Front Cover Image

The blessing of the new borehole at Kikonge.

Kikonge is a small trading center about 2 or 3 kilometers east of Kyengeza on the road to Kampala. Fr David blessed the borehole donated by the Sisters of Mary of Mount Carmel. Mother Michaela, the Superior General of the Sisters, and Sr Elizabeth operate the pump for the very first time. All present are full of delight and gratitude for the clean, fresh, cool water from God's earth.

Back Cover Image

Fr David visits with Sr Antonia and her Ebimuli (The Flowers) choir as they practice for next Sunday's Mass under a shady mango tree.

Sing to the Lord a new song.

Sing to the Lord, all the earth.

Sing to the Lord, bless his name.

Announce his salvation day after day.

Tell God's glory among the nations.

Among all peoples, God's marvelous deeds.

—Psalm 96

Contents

Foreword

By Father Adam Gregory Gonzales

In 1924 the Anglo-Irish Province of Discalced Carmelite Friars began sending many young, vital, and faith-filled Friars to a distant place called California. Missionaries?

Yes! These young men were from the life they knew in Ireland to a relatively unknown country to spread their love for Christ and the spirituality of Carmel. So, I say, without reservation, that the California-Arizona Province of Discalced Carmelite Friars contains the missionary spirit! It was the Irish Fathers and Brothers who instilled this in us.

Seventy-eight years later, in 2002, it was one of these sons of Ireland who would move to Uganda to begin our mission. Although Fr. David already had experience with the Carmelite mission in Kenya, he was now planting roots for us in a place called Kyengeza in Eastern Africa. It was there that he fearlessly led our Friars, our Carmelite Sisters, and Carmelite Seculars into the unknown. You are about to read his story. As you do, please keep Fr. David and all the Friars of our Province in your prayer because the story is not finished. Other Friars have now taken up the work.

When I visit our Friars in Uganda, it is clear how Fr. David's efforts have borne fruit. We now have a thriving community of native Ugandans, and more are coming. As we see in the life of Saint Teresa of Jesus and the development of the renewed Carmel, it takes just one person to start something beautiful for God. Holy Mother Church and our Province owe an outstanding debt of gratitude to Fr. David for starting something beautiful for God in Uganda. On behalf of the Province, I thank Fr. David for his excellent work in Africa and this invaluable historical record. As the "Vintage of Grace" (the recorded history of the founding of the California-Arizona Province by Fr. Edward Leahy, O.C.D.) has become a treasured classic of our Province, I believe that 'African Memories': "Come Back Tomorrow" will take its rightful place in our hearts and on our Carmelite bookshelves.

Fr Adam Gonzales OCD (Provincial)

Introduction

The title of this book comes from my first visit to the Post Office in the town of Mityana (20 minutes from our parish), which is in the Mubende district of central Uganda. Mityana is where the Bishops of the Anglican and Catholic dioceses have their residences and administrative offices. The Anglican Bishop has the title "Bishop of Mityana," distinguishing him from the Catholic Bishop we call the "Bishop of Kiyinda-Mityana." "Kiyinda" is the name of the Bishop's residence, the Catechetical Center, the administrative offices, the Cathedral, the Catholic cemetery, and the shrine to the local Ugandan martyrs. The Carmelite Nuns' monastery is also there at Kiyinda.

Mityana is a small busy town of approximately 5,000 inhabitants. Apart from the beautiful Catholic Cathedral, there are few prominent buildings in the city. However, if you proceed down the main street, you might be surprised to find two banks, an internet café, a supermarket, the Kolping House hotel, the post office and, the somewhat remote police station. Since there is no direct mail delivery to residences in Uganda, it is necessary to pick up your mail at a rented box in the local Post Office. My first visit to the post office was to get a P.O. Box Number where we could pick up our mail, and of course, to purchase some Uganda stamps.

Uganda Post Office

There was no trouble getting the box number—pay the small annual fee and verify your name. Following that, I was shocked to hear that they did not have any stamps today! The young lady attendant told me quite casually, "Come back tomorrow." Thinking I did not hear her correctly, I said, "I beg your pardon." She repeated her original statement, loud and clear, and returned to her chores. Still reeling with unbelief, I realized I was not at the Oakville Post Office in the Napa Valley of California. I was now in Africa!

Leaving the building and getting into my truck, I muttered to myself several times, "Come back tomorrow! Come back tomorrow! How about that" and then, laughing, "if ever I think of writing something on the Ugandan mission, at least I have a title"!

That was almost 20 years ago! Memories are not history. They are not as precise as documented accounts of past events, yet they color the past with human warmth and often with vague imperfections. Many might suggest that it is too soon to compile a history of the Ugandan Mission, which began in 2002, but it is not too soon to put memories on paper.

When we try to remember, we find happy and sad memories; sentiment enters quickly, sometimes pain and tears and, even with some selective memories, a hesitancy to explore.

Although memory focuses on the past, we can also ask or promise to remember in the future. The plea of the "good thief" on Calvary to Jesus comes to mind "Remember me when you come into your Kingdom," which called forth an astonishing reply from the Lord. That same plea has been prayed and sung about with great confidence down through the years. The Lord Himself also commanded His apostles, "Do this in memory of me." The Church fulfills this injunction every time we celebrate the Holy Sacrifice of the Mass. What Jesus did at the Last Supper is mysteriously and wonderfully made present by the priest's words over the bread and wine on the altar.

Someone does need to write down significant events in our families—human and religious families—to help us realize that we are not isolated individuals but members of a more significant association and a more outstanding design than anything merely human. May these memories of the African mission of our Province recall and inspire others to rejoice in their Baptismal call to mission. May they give honor and glory to the God who is always at work in His people.

Let me also give thanks and acknowledge the accounts of other members of our California-Arizona Province who have written well about the Province we all treasure:

"Vintage of Grace" by Fr. Edward Leahy OCD – Discalced Carmelites in California 1923–1982. (1983, Teresian Publications)

"Carmelites Among Miners" by Fr. Anastasio Font OCD – Discalced Carmelites in Arizona. (1991, Carmelite Institute of Spirituality)

"Memoirs" by Fr. Patrick Perjes OCD – an unpublished personal account of the life of this Hungarian missionary, a onetime P.O.W. in Uganda. (1993)

"Updates from Uganda" many written by Fr. Colm Stone OCD and compiled by our Mission Office secretary, Helga Nice.

"Carmelite Mission Newsletter," written by Fr. David Costello and Fr. Reginald McSweeney and compiled by Mission Office secretaries Helga Nice and Bill Zdanoski, 2002–2018.

Fr. Edward Leahy   Fr. Anastasio Font   Fr. Patrick Perjes

1
How It Began

"halfway across the globe"?

In May 1993, at the Provincial Chapter - the gathering of Superiors and delegates to elect new leaders and deal with vital interests of our California/Arizona (Calif-Az in short) Province - we received a letter from the General of our Order, Fr. Phillip Sainz de Baranda. He invited us to go to Kenya to take charge of the International House of formation in Nairobi. That house was founded and built under the inspiration of Fr. Phillip himself, a native of Spain and a great missionary in South America. It was designated to serve the needs of English-speaking African Carmelite students. The Generalate staffed it by selecting individual Carmelites from different Provinces but now wanted one of the American Provinces to assume responsibility. Fr. Phillip sent his letter to the three American Provinces of Washington, Oklahoma, and Calif-Az to set up this new arrangement. Our Province of Calif-Az was the first to hold its Chapter that year and consequently got the first chance to say "Yes" or "No."

We considered the invitation prayerfully. We listened to the account of one of our members, Fr. David Centner, who had ministered in Nairobi for about a year and gave a favorable impression of the situation. During the break following his talk, some of us informally commented, "it sounds pretty attractive; a golf course and a racetrack (horse racing); not bad at all"!

The Chapter's decision, our response, included an expression of gratitude to the General for inviting us. Still, as a new, young Province, we did not have the personnel to take on such a big responsibility. Among ourselves, we felt that one of the other Provinces – Washington to be precise – had more significant numbers and would be better able to rise to the opportunity. We offered to help in whatever way we could. At this stage, I presented myself as a volunteer for Nairobi. Our Provincial, Fr. Gerald Werner, duly notified the General of our decision, and we waited for the other Provinces' decisions. Sure enough, the Washington province responded positively; the Oklahoma province, like us, stated that they could not take it on but were willing to help in whatever way possible. Fr. Gerald, our Provincial, communicated with the Washington Provincial and informed him of my offer to volunteer. He seemed to be happy with that offer.

However, I heard nothing further from the Washington Province, and I began to think that their leadership was not accepting my offer. Yet I was happy I had volunteered and said to myself – "good try, Costello"! Then, out of the blue in March 1994, Fr. Gerald surprised me with the question, "Are you still interested in going to Nairobi"? I was taken aback and asked for a week to reconsider it; I prayed and discerned and returned to the Provincial with a positive reply.

As preparation for Missionary work, I attended the "Maryknoll Preparation Course" at St Mary's, Moraga (south of San

Francisco). Fr. Larry Daniels and Bro. Gilmary of the Washington Province had already taken a similar course for prospective missionaries in Texas. The Moraga course was a wonderful experience. Thirty-five men and women from many congregations attended the course to explore their call to mission in foreign lands. The presenters were the Maryknoll team, assisted by others - psychologists, theologians, and spiritual directors - with fruitful interaction among the participants themselves.

Not everyone discerned their 'call to mission.' However, I was happy to be affirmed in my decision. At the ripe old age of 57, I was preparing for a new life in Kenya – medical check-ups, vaccinations, and the inevitable interrogations. Some expressed surprise and anger when I resigned from my position as Oakville Superior; another lay friend gave his opinion in a somewhat sarcastic tone, "Where did you get that crazy idea"? But for the most part, it was an affirmation, good wishes, farewell songs, poems, prayerful commissioning services and, even a few fake tears by my Carmelite Brothers on the morning I was leaving for the airport. A Christmas vacation in Ireland was the icing on the cake, even though it snowed on St Stephen's Day (December 26th). My brother, Fr Jimmy, and relatives in Ireland were surprised at my Kenyan adventure but fully supported it.

LIFE IN KENYA
(See maps of Africa and Kenya on page 203)

The community of friars in Nairobi was happy to welcome me to their ranks. Fr. Larry Daniels from Wisconsin was the community Superior, and there were two others from the Washington Province, Brothers Gilmary and Bernard. Other senior community members included: Fr. Tom Curran, from the Anglo-Irish Province

– an old friend of mine, Fr. Rafael Mendoza from Spain, and Fr Valerian from India. One of my first requests to take a three-month intensive course in the native language, Swahili, was strangely not granted by the gracious and generous Superior. He stated, "This is an international community, and since English is our common language, there is no need for Swahili! You will pick up enough spontaneously." I did, in fact – a few words like "Jambo" (hello), "Assante sana" (thank you), "hakuna pesa" (I have no money), etc. Later, I regretted that I had not insisted with my Superior because this Bantu language, Swahili, would have made learning Luganda, the language of Uganda and the Bantu group, much more manage-able. Still, in truth, Uganda was not yet on the radar.

Kenya is located north of Tanzania in Eastern Africa.

The student community in Nairobi was made up of young men from Nigeria, Malawi, Tanzania (Indian by nationality), and some new vocations from Kenya, the nucleus of that future Carmelite region. My first assignment as "Vocations Director" dealt with the many applications coming in by mail. Answering these letters, helping the various correspondents discern the call of God in their lives, and organizing vocational "Live-ins" were all exciting ways to get in touch with the youth of Kenya and to get a glimpse of God's work in their lives.

The sad news of the death of Fr. Edward Leahy, OCD at Oakville, California, reached us shortly after I arrived in Nairobi. He had been a great leader in the Calif-Az province, a friend of mine, and a staunch affirmer of the Carmelite missionary spirit. He was deeply involved in the loss of our parish in Encino and the founder of our two houses in Northern California, Oakville and San Jose. I was the chief celebrant at his memorial Mass and in the homily recalled Fr. Edward's favorite well-known hymn:

"Be thou my Vision, O Lord of my heart
Naught be all else save that thou art.
Thou my best thought in the day and the night
Waking or sleeping, thy presence my light."

May he enjoy the vision of God in heaven and the fullness of life forever.

I settled in gradually, but not without occasional darkness and doubt. In one of these moments, I recalled Fr. Gerald's gracious offer, "Would you like to try it out for three months before you make the final decision"? My reply was a sincere "No, I'm going to stay for the full term of three years"! But in these times of darkness, I was tested and could only come up with a kind of a low-grade humility, "I cannot go back on what I promised"! Letters from home were consoling and affirming in my struggles, but above all, the phone calls from friends boosted me. That was before the mobile phone era, and it wasn't easy to get through to Kenya by phone. Sometimes it wasn't easy to find me in our sprawling monastery with only a few phones available. The human voice of friends is truly a blessing from God.

As I gradually became more settled, other ministry jobs came my way – Student Master, Retreat Master, assistant librarian, and an invitation to teach in the Spirituality department of the nearby Tangaza College, Nairobi, where our students studied Theology. Fr. Tom Curran taught history there and was instrumental in setting up the Spirituality Department and Course. These assignments were challenges, but they were also opportunities to enter the African experience fully. It was indeed a time of grace and continued until 2000.

A TASTE OF UGANDA

Towards the end of my time in Kenya, Fr. Jeremiah Fitzpatrick, OCD from the Anglo-Irish Province was one of our General Councillors in Rome. Part of his ministry was to visit the Carmelite Nuns in Uganda. Being a fellow Irishman and a friend from my early days of teaching in Ireland, he invited me to come along with him to Uganda. This visit was my first contact with the "Pearl of Africa," as Winston Churchill described the country of Uganda. Mother Benedicta, Prioress of the Carmelite Nuns warmly welcomed us and brought us to meet the local Bishop of Kiyinda-Mityana Diocese, Joseph Mukwaya. Both the Carmelite Nuns and the Bishop had invited the Friars to come to Uganda. Both were very hopeful and very sincere about their invitation. Mother Benedicta also arranged a meeting with the Cardinal Archbishop of

Kampala, Cardinal Wamala. The Cardinal was a great friend of Mother Benedicta since he had been the first Bishop of Kiyinda-Mityana before being assigned to Kampala. (Our eventual mission of Kyengeza lies about 50 kilometers west of Kampala and then about 20 kilometers from Mityana).

Our meeting with the Cardinal was charming. He is a real gentleman, easy to converse with, and he offered us a choice of tea or coffee while he enjoyed his preferred morning snack of popcorn! He also had a specific offer for us to consider. It was a large Conference Center in Kampala; he hoped to have it renovated and functioning again in the archdiocese. We had already seen the place as we visited a nearby Jesuit house with Mother Benedicta. I was not too impressed because of the large size of the building. Much work would be needed to repair it and get it into shape for any real ministry. That did not match my idea of missionary work among God's people. Besides that, the road leading up to it was gutted and full of potholes which left a negative impression. I also wondered why the Cardinal had not asked the nearby Jesuit community to take on the project. Maybe he did, and perhaps the Jesuits did not bite. Bishop Mukwaya's offer was more attractive, even if it meant serving God's people out in the bush!

On the return flight to Nairobi, we reviewed our visit to Uganda; the question of a foundation of the Friars inevitably surfaced once more. I suggested to Fr. Jerry that he might ask the Calif-Az province to consider making a foundation in Uganda. Then, I added that I would be willing to be part of this new venture.

Armed with an invitation letter from the current Superior General, Fr. Camillo Maccise, Fr Jerry lost no time consulting the Californian Provincial, Fr. Gerald Werner. With newly elected Provincial, Fr. Stephen Watson, Fr Gerald took practical steps to discern God's will for the province regarding a new mission. Many were favorable, but others had doubts about having enough personnel to take on this new venture. Fr. Stephen met with Bishop Mukwaya on his visits to Africa in Mityana. I accompanied him. The Bishop was keen to open a new "Millennium" (2000) parish and had it well outlined for Kyengeza. Keeping in mind the hesitations back in the home region, Fr. Stephen was cautious about making a definite commitment.

Map of Uganda showing Kyengeza location.

Mother Benedicta, Bishop Mukwaya, Len Powers, and Fr. David Costello

The Bishop and I were firmly in favor, even though in a private moment with me, Bishop Mukwaya remarked, "Were we too hard on Steve"? He enjoyed the discussion and banter and respected the Provincial's concerns.

The Province was building and funding a new House of Studies at Mount Angel in Oregon. Fr. Stephen, following on the suggestions of the Provincial Council, was negotiating with one of the Indian Provinces for a loan of some Indian friars to help the personnel situation in the Province. He successfully got three fine friars - Fr. Datius, going to El Carmelo, Redlands, Fr. Justin, coming to our Santa Cruz Parish in Tucson, Arizona, and Fr Xavier, taking up residence at our House of Prayer in Oakville.

I revisited Uganda with a lay volunteer friend, Len Powers, working with us in Nairobi. This visit responded to an invitation by the Banakaroli Brothers, a native Ugandan congregation of Bro. Joseph Yiga, Bishop Mukwaya's chauffeur, for talks about Carmelite spirituality at their General Chapter.

While giving my spirituality lectures to the Brothers, Len explored the Church scene around Mityana and made friends with local priests. One of these was Fr. John Vianney Mwezi, who later served with us at St. Kizito's parish, Kyengeza. Fr. John Vianney's priestly vocation inspired him to join the Blessed Sacrament Fathers. He came to the United States for part of his religious formation in that community and visited Len's home parish at St. Apollinaris in Napa, California.

St. Apollinaris Catholic Church, Napa, California

Len's missionary spirit did not end at St. Apollinaris, as he is a member of the Oakville OCDS group. At present, he is Mission Director for his parish and a great leader in the mission's Recycling Program with another staunch missionary couple from the same parish, Jeanette and Tom Bennett.

In California, Fr. Stephen presented his Council with the findings from his visit to Uganda and promoted the mission to the Province. The Provincial and his Council agreed to take on the Mission. On my return to California in 2000, I set about establishing a Mission office to provide for the temporal needs of the mission, with Helga Nice as a competent volunteer secretary. Helga and her husband Frank were good friends of the Oakville community (in the Napa Valley), and they knew me well.

FINANCES

We needed funds to begin and sustain our new missionary venture. The project of building a new House of Studies in Oregon already made considerable demands on the limited financial resources of the Province. Hence the Mission Office fund-raising efforts were essential to the Uganda project. The Mission Newsletter and various Mission appeals were also ways of spreading the word about our new venture. The very first Mission Appeal at the Carmelite Monastery Chapel at Carmel-by–the-Sea in California was a great start and surprised the Mission Director with the sum of $3,000.00.

The Mission Director continued to reach out to the various dioceses in California and Nevada and was permitted to make Mission appeals at some of their parishes. The parishioners were invariably supportive and generous. It was also an exciting time for the Mission Director to get to know the Diocesan clergy and make friends with many of them.

Making a budget for the first year of the actual mission was another interesting experience since we estimated the costs from a California standpoint and eventually found out that the prices were not so high in Uganda. That left us in good shape financially, and there was no new burden on the Provincial funds. Other Mission Appeals outside of California and Nevada, surprising support from Ireland, and the connection with Carmelite Mission Directors in Ireland and England were bonus blessings.

Some of the donations that flowed in were memorable:

- the few dollars that came in regularly from a man whose address was "General Delivery,"
- the interest and energy of school children in helping the cause,
- the crumbled, somewhat soiled check that was given to me after one of my parish appeals and turned out to be $350.00 and never bounced,
- the startling sum of $25,000.00 from a non-Catholic lady

who had come to see me about family issues and whose husband committed suicide, but left her a big Life Insurance, of which she gave a tithe to the Mission,

- the most significant and generous Mission Appeal parish contribution from the Vietnamese parish in San Jose,
- the establishment and outstanding support of the "Wine to Water" foundation to provide clean water for our people.

All these and many others supported and sustained the mission, eased the burden of fundraising, but also glorified God by their care for God's people in Uganda. May the Lord continue to reward each one of the benefactors of our Mission.

The idea of a mission in Africa from the new and comparatively young Calif-Az Province caught the attention of many, and great support came in from many people, especially the Secular Carmelites and the Carmelite Nuns. However, personnel remained a difficulty. Bishop Mukwaya had the proposed "millennium" parish of St. Kizito, Kyengeza, lined up for us, hoping that we would come in the first year of the new millennium. But missionaries for the harvest were not forthcoming. Some friars had an aversion to a mission in Africa – "halfway across the world"? Others were more sympathetic, stating, "if I were ten years younger, I would go," and some were tied down by leadership positions in the province.

SEARCHING FOR A TEAM

I prayed and organized a retreat for possible candidates to discern their missionary call. Only a small group attended, but the surprise volunteer that stood out was a Secular Carmelite nurse from Sacramento – Lillian Kelly. As a public health nurse with missionary experience in Nepal, she was a strong candidate – but would a woman be accepted?

I also contacted a Brother from the Washington Province, Bernard Olk, whom I knew well from our time together in Nairobi. Bernard was young and strong and willing to try his missionary vocation once more. Amazingly, we now had three possible candidates, and thankfully they were all accepted by the Provincial and his Council. St. Teresa of Avila was delighted to have "a Friar and a Half" (St. John of the Cross and Fr. Antonio) for the first foundation of the Discalced Carmelite Friars, at Duruelo, in Spain. The three of us were grateful to God and excited to share in this new Carmelite adventure. The usual preparations included medical check-ups, passports, flight arrangements, and special Commissioning of the new missionaries to service the Gospel in Uganda. It was exciting for those involved but somewhat mysterious and doubtful for others; the mantra of doubt continued - "how can we develop a mission halfway across the world." Yet as well as this, another Friar, Fr. Colm Stone, was showing serious interest in the Mission - the missionary call was still alive, thanks be to God.

CALIFORNIA MISSION SITES

Part of my preparation was spiritual, which consisted of a pilgrimage to the Californian mission sites founded by Fr. Junipero Serra OFM. On the next page is a photo of Mission San Luis Rey, Oceanside in Southern California, founded in 1798.

I began at Mission Dolores in San Francisco. And I made my way down south through the state to the missions in Santa Clara, San Miguel, San Luis Obispo, Carmel, Santa Barbara, Ventura, San Juan Capistrano, San Diego, and back to San Gabriel.

Mission San Luis Rey in Oceanside, California was founded in 1798.

The entire journey was delightful and inspiring, especially the last two places where I had lived close by during my days in Redlands and Alhambra, but they had never touched me so profoundly in earlier years. It was not all prayer – there were visits with friends, words of encouragement, and even a day at the races and a few movies on African themes – "Out of Africa," "The Lion King," as well as the classic, "The Mission." Ray McAnally, a former teacher from my younger days in Dublin, starred in that movie. Another teacher from former school days in Castlemartyr, Fr. Jerome Lantry, who served as Provincial of both the Irish and Californian provinces, called to congratulate me, wish me well, and tell me what a blessing it was for our Province to open its own mission – a pleasant surprise and a genuine affirmation of our missionary venture.

"TUUTUNO" – WE ARE HERE

"Tuutuno" is a response of the Ugandan martyrs to the king when he demanded to know where these Christians were. They did not make any attempt to hide their faith by replying vigorously "Tuutuno" = "We are here."

I left California in February 2002 to go as a missionary to Uganda. I took my first Lariam tablet to protect against that dreaded African disease - malaria. Lillian Kelly and I met in London and traveled together to Entebbe. Bernard's flight from Washington did not arrive until the next day. Fr. Lawrence OFM Cap. Regional Superior of the Capuchins in Uganda welcomed us warmly and provided gracious hospitality at their Postulant house close to the Entebbe airport. I knew him from my visits to Uganda, where he was the Pastor of Busungu, the adjoining parish to Kyengeza. The next day, Bro. Joseph, the chauffeur and secretary to the Bishop, and Msgr. Paul Nkombya, the diocese's Vicar General, arrived in separate vehicles to transport us to Bishop Mukwaya's house. We stayed there for approximately a week to relax and enjoy the Bishop's hospitality. After some formal introductions, he enquired about our families; he was fascinated when Bernard told us that he was one of nine children. The Bishop questioned him further - "that is eleven in your family... is your mother African"?

Bishop Mukwaya, small in stature, gracious and friendly, seemed to enjoy our company. One evening, after a late supper, he invited me to join him in the T.V. room to watch a Premier League soccer game between Arsenal and Liverpool. Later I learned that the Bishop was a "tough soccer player" in his younger days in the seminary. He was an ardent fan of Arsenal and questioned which team I supported. To my answer, "Newcastle," he immediately countered with "why Newcastle"? To explain my soccer allegiance, I had to tell him how a former Bishop of Newcastle, Joseph McCormack, was a relative of my mother. Duly unimpressed, he continued to cheer for his team, "the Gunners."

On different days we celebrated Masses at the Bishop's house, the Cathedral, and the Carmelite Nun's chapel. We also met with Fr. Kasimbi Mbaaga Tuzende, the pastor of St Kizito's, Kyengeza. That parish was already open as a Jubilee parish of the Millennium and would be our eventual destination. It was a great joy to visit the parish and meet with the assistant parish priest, Fr. Matia Lutalo, and one of the parish leaders, Mark Gingo. The Uganda expression of welcome, "You are most welcome," was used repeatedly, followed by "feel at home"! This Ugandan expression of welcome, "you are most welcome," "feel at home," is undoubtedly an invitation to be at ease, to know you belong here, that you are safe, that we love and appreciate you – it is like that well-known phrase "home is where the heart is." But for most of us, our first home is where we were born and spent our early years.

For me, those words, although sincere, seemed a bit forced or overdone, but as the days and years passed, I realized how genuine they were and how authentically they expressed Ugandan hospitality. It is crucial at this stage to state that this Uganda invitation was not the first of its kind to our province and that God is always calling us to new ways of serving Him and His people.

EARLIER CALLS TO MISSION
Other Carmelites had arrived as missionaries to Africa before us.

- The Carmelite Nuns, whenever they pioneer the Carmelite presence in a new land will often appeal to the Generalate of our Order to send some Carmelite Friars to assist them with their Carmelite spirituality. Our Carmelite Nuns in Uganda did that on many occasions when the General or his representative visited them but in so far as I know never appealed directly to our Province.

- In 1978, when the Calif-Az region received its status as a "Regional Vicariate" – a stage of greater independence on the road to becoming a fully established Province - Fr. Patrick Sugrue, OCD was our Provincial leader and, another Patrick - Mootherhill by surname, from India, - was on the General Council or Definitory of the Order. They knew one another from their student days at the Teresianum in Rome. Fr. Mootherhill appealed to Fr. Sugrue to take on a mission in Nigeria, but Fr. Sugrue stated that a small, newly formed Region could not take on such a big project. Fr. Mootherhill was persistent, and a kind of a diplomatic tug-of-war ensued between the two leaders. In fact, at one stage, even two or three of our men were named in the 'rumor mill' as assigned to Nigeria and specifically to Enugu! Fr. John Melka, the first native Californian to become a Carmelite, told me a slightly different story. The two friars involved were John himself and Fr Hugo Townsend, from the English Region. The General Councillor told them to prepare for the mission to Taiwan and Nigeria. Furthermore, Fr. Cyprian, a greatly loved friar ministering in Arizona, was also mentioned for the Nigerian mission. Eventually, the Anglo-Irish Province took on the Nigerian task, and it is now a flourishing Region soon expected to become a fully-fledged Province. It is doing so well that now the Anglo-Irish Province is being referred to as a mission of Nigeria!

- Fr. Patrick Perjes OCD, a Hungarian Carmelite, was on mission in Bagdad, Iraq, in the early years of World War II. Being a member of an axis country, he was taken prisoner by the British invading forces and sent to Uganda as a P.O.W. There, Fr. Patrick made friends with his British

captors and moved around with some freedom. Visiting the various mission centers of the White Fathers (whose official title is Missionaries of Africa but because of their white robes were known as the White Fathers). At their Konge mission, he became acquainted with Fr. Karoli Lutwama, the son of a native chieftain and the first native Ugandan to join the White Fathers. He was well known as the "First black, White Father." He offered some property to Fr. Patrick, property from his father's estate to start a foundation of the Carmelites in Uganda. But Fr. Patrick was trying to get a passport to move out of Africa to a safer destination. Eventually, he did succeed, stayed for a short while in Ireland, and then moved on to serve with the Spanish Carmelites in Arizona. That put him in the Calif-Az Province and ended his days in Oakville, California, where I was the local Superior. Before his death in 1993, he completed an interesting "Memoirs" of his travels around the globe as a Carmelite Missionary. God rest his soul.

CARMELITE MISSIONS IN AFRICA

During his pontificate, St. Pope Paul VI urged the traditional religious Orders, including the Discalced Carmelite Friars, to bring their Charisms to the new Churches of Africa and establish their presence on that continent. The Discalced Carmelite's response has been to go to the following places in Africa

- The Congo—directly under the Generalate sponsorship
- Malawi—a mission of the Navarre Province of Spain

- Central African Republic—an assignment of the Genoa Province
- Nigeria—a mission of the Anglo-Irish Province
- Kenya—a mission of the Eastern (USA) Province of Washington
- Tanzania—a mission from the Karnataka—Goa (India) Province
- Uganda—a mission of the California-Arizona Province since 2002.

2

"Who Is David?"

"It's a long way to Tipperary..."

In Ireland, I was born in Tipperary town, a county of a similar name, to Kathleen and William Costello in 1936. I was the second son of these not-so-young parents, born a year and a half after my older brother, Jimmy. My father was a plumber. His big white sign with bright green letters, in his workshop, proclaimed, "Plumber and Sanitary Engineer"! Unfortunately, in 1939 he died of a duodenal ulcer in a Dublin hospital where they could not stop the bleeding. It was tragic for the family newly settled in the small agricultural town of about 4,000 people. But my mother was courageous and persevering in her faith in raising her two sons. She wanted above all to give them a good education, which at that time in Ireland, and for her, meant to complete high school or have a secondary education. But life was not easy, yet it was happy and simple. She had the support of her extended Catholic family. She was creative in finding stay-at-home work situations for the family.

The marching song "It's a long way to Tipperary" was viral in

24

the first World War for the Irish soldiers in the British army, but it is more romantic than nationalistic. A native Tipperary person would prefer "Slievenamon," or even more so, a local town's person would choose "Tipperary Hills for me." I spent many happy days around the hills on the north side of this agricultural area. I broke my leg trying to jump over a sizeable hole, and we played all kinds of games in that beautiful place. On the southern side, the Galtee mountains were the great attraction that led to the rich land of the Golden Vale. Later in life, I would enjoy the rolling hills of Uganda called the "Pearl of Africa" by Winston Churchill and remember my native home.

One of my recent remembered events from childhood was being with my mother in Coman's grocery store. As in many small Irish shops, there was a collection box for the Missions on the counter. I discovered that this one came alive when some coins were dropped in it – the diminutive figure of the black baby bowed his head up and down for a few minutes in gratitude. "Mammie," I pleaded with her, "can I have a penny for the Black Babies"?

She gave it to me willingly, and I was thrilled to see the black baby's bobbing head and smiling face in response to my little donation. Perhaps that was the seed of my love for Africa and my first memory of that land.

CASTLEMARTYR, CO. CORK
(*See Map of Ireland on page 201*)
(*See Map of Ireland on page 201*)

Fast forward to the visit of a Carmelite priest, Fr. Joseph McElhinney, to our Christian Brother's school promoting vocations to the priesthood. In our Primary school class of about 50 students, twelve of us raised our hands, saying that we were interested in becoming priests. Fr. Joseph afterward consulted with the Brothers, our teachers, and visited the homes of some of us. When he was leaving town and going to the bus, I accompanied him, carrying his small suitcase; he thanked me and gave me a "half-a-crown" for assisting him – a princely sum for a young boy in those days!

His invitation to us was to come for secondary school to the Carmelite College or Juniorate at Castlemartyr, Co. Cork, (east of Cork city) and possibly move on from there to study for the priesthood. It was an exciting prospect and adventure for a twelve-year-old. The "college," as it was called at that time, is in a lovely little village, where the ruins of an old castle stand out prominently alongside the college buildings and a small lake. The student body numbered about 75, with twelve newcomers from various parts of Ireland in the first-year class. The Carmelite Priests and Brothers, and the lay teachers, were all good men; they never pressured us to join the Order, but in fact, many of the students did become Carmelites. For the most part, it was a happy and carefree experience living in a small boarding school, yet we all looked forward to returning home for the long summer vacation and the shorter ones at Christmas and Easter.

Father David plays football as a boy in school.

On one occasion, I remember feeling sad after the long summer in Tipperary and yet delighted to be back with my school pals. We all went to the chapel for night prayers and what seemed to be a long period of silent prayer. As I gazed out the vast windows of the chapel surveying the playing fields, the handball alley, and the tennis court, I prayed to myself, "I miss home,… but this is also my home." On many occasions, I also wondered at the Latin words inscribed on the altar cloth, "Magister adest et vocat te." (The Master is here and calls you).

In the final year of our course, we all began to think seriously about our future after the last school exams. I had always had a strong desire to become a priest, but now I needed to know more about the Carmelites. I came across a recently published book written by an Irish Carmelite on the missions in the Philippines entitled "A Man Shall Scatter" by Fr. Sebastian Buckley, OCD, himself a graduate of Castlemartyr.

I was fascinated by his account of the mission and especially by the dust jacket that pictured a Carmelite priest in his habit with a hard hat, setting out on a mission journey on horseback with his Mass kit, plus a crucifix under his belt. I imagined a revolver that I figured must be somewhere. No doubts assailed my mind; I was convinced and ready to go! I cried out with delight, "That's life; that's what I want"!

When I returned home that summer, I got a huge surprise. My brother, Jimmy, had finished secondary school a year before me, was working and helping to provide for our little family. Mother announced to me, "Jimmy is going to Thurles"! Thurles was the well-known diocesan seminary in our area, so I knew what that meant; he had decided to go on for the diocesan priesthood. I was dumbfounded and blurted out, "What will happen to you, Mammie"? She just smiled and gently replied, "don't worry about me. I will be all right." She was happy that her two sons wanted to be priests. The Gospel story of Jesus observing the poor widow putting her two coins in the temple collection has often reminded me of my own widowed mother's generosity. She was delighted to give her sons to God and was present joyfully at their ordinations in Thurles in 1961 and Rome in 1962.

SIBLING RIVALRY

Jimmy was always the 'big' brother; he was the leader in all activities, and I was always trying to catch up with him. Both of us loved sports, but he was the determined fighter type and, for that, got the nickname "Slogger." I was known as "Slogger's little brother" and got my nickname, an abbreviation from the Gaelic for David – Daithi – which became "Dots." One of the Church activities that Jimmy got involved in was the "Legion of Mary," which was flourishing in Ireland and had a solid apostolic and missionary aspect. One of his friends in that group was a young priest, Fr. Bobby Bradshaw, who organized a missionary trip to Scotland for the group. Later in his life, Fr. Bobby went to Iceland as an envoy of the Legion and later to Krasnoyarsk in Siberia. Fr Jimmy decided to visit his friend Fr. Bobby and his fellow Legionaries in Siberia.

Unfortunately, Fr. Bobby was in poor health and died during Fr. Jimmy's visit in 1993.

Jimmy had the daunting task of bringing Fr. Bobby's body back home to Ireland for burial in his native Tipperary. It was a fascinating saga to accomplish this task – dealing with Russian bureaucracy, travel, climate, unscrupulous officials, and a host of other problems. But he did it and recounted it to me many times. I urged him to write down the details of this adventure, but he has not done it yet!

Jimmy was ordained for the Diocese of Southwark in London and spent six years on that mission before returning to the Limerick Diocese to be closer to my mother in her later years. He served in various parishes in Limerick and is retired now in his last parish, St Peter and Paul's in Bruff.

"Novitiate" is the term used to describe the first stage of formation, required by the Church, for religious men and women who are called Novices. It is often preceded by a "Postulancy" period of various lengths of time, in which the individual is requesting admittance to the order or congregation. The Novitiate time begins with the "Clothing" of the new member in the religious habit of the congregation and continues for at least one year. In this "spiritual year," the novice experiences community's life in the style embodied in the life and teaching of its founder and the Rule and Constitutions of the congregation. This time ends with the "First or Simple Profession of Vows" – poverty, chastity, and obedience – and then continues for a further period of three to five years before "Final or Solemn Profession of Vows." This second stage often coincides with college or theology studies for those preparing for the priesthood.

Before entering the Carmelite Novitiate, I felt the need to check in with my home parish priest in Tipperary. Archdeacon

Nicholas Cooke was a good friend of Jimmy and a promoter of his vocation to the diocesan priesthood. The Archdeacon had been President of the Seminary in Thurles and had a stake in providing recruits. When I visited him, he was open and definite that I should join my brother and go to Thurles. But I was just as unequivocal in replying, "No! I'm staying with the Carmelites; they know me, and I like them"! He gave a grudging approval but reminded me that I needed a reference from my parish priest. When I told him they did not advise me about it, he reacted, "strange people! They don't know the proper procedure"! He did, however, say that I would need it and that he would give me one. I was happy to get it, but I was never asked for it when I arrived at the Novitiate; I kept it in my suitcase for a few years until I made my final Profession in the Carmelite Order.

Jimmy, on his part, claims that I was the one trying to allure him to join the Carmelites and that my approach was, "join the Carmelites and see the world"! I must have spoken about the Filipino attraction and hope. Despite this different account, we always kept close to one another, and he treated me very well whenever I came home on vacation. We went to sporting events; he helped me stay in touch with relatives and planned great trips abroad. We journeyed to Scotland, where we visited Iona and played golf

Here I am as a young Carmelite student with my seminarian brother, Jimmy.

at St. Andrews, to Austria to celebrate Sr. Antonia's Silver Jubilee, to Valencia in Spain when Pope Benedict celebrated Family Life and many other enjoyable trips. He came to the U.S.A., Kenya, and Uganda and got in his share of seeing the world as well as supporting his brother's Carmelite vocation.

DREAM INTERRUPTED

My dream of going to the Philippines remained strong during my years of study at the International College in Rome. The American students from the Washington and Oklahoma provinces envied us, Irish Carmelites, because as ordained men, California, a mission of the Anglo-Irish Province, was a possible destination. That merely affirmed my desire for the Philippines! However, after my ordination in 1962, I was assigned to the House of Studies in Dublin. Then after three years of teaching, the Provincial at that time, Fr. Reginald McSweeney, called me to his office and, in the style of that time, told me, "we are sending you to California 'on loan' for two years." There was no discussion, no consultation, and humble obedience to the Provincial Superior was expected. When I shared the news with my brother Carmelites in the community, they laughed aloud at the "on loan" proviso. Shortly afterward, I happened to meet the Provincial and recounted to him the reaction of my brothers. He was upset at these reported reactions and somewhat offended, but clearly and decisively restated his original decision "That's it; it's down in black and white"!

I was happy in California; I fell in love with the Golden State, especially with my ministry for eleven years at El Carmelo Retreat House in Redlands (sixty miles east of Los Angeles and some 40 miles west of Palm Springs) in Southern California. The "loan" became permanent. I duly forgot about the mission to the Philippines, but God did not forget about the dream of my youth! In

1993 the call to the missions was re-awakened, and, in 1994, I was discerning the call to Kenya.

Fr. David Costello with his brother, Fr. Jim Costello,
who travelled from Ireland for the celebration of David's Golden Jubilee.

The discernment developed as follows; almost a year after my offer for Kenya, there was no word from the Washington province. Then, our Provincial, Fr. Gerald Werner, gave me the news that they were still interested and if I were still willing to go. It was a jolt to my state of mind at that time, and I asked for a week to think it over again. I consulted my Spiritual Director – Fr. Dare Morgan S.J. – who lived in Sacramento. We made an appointment for lunch, and I told Fr. Dare my story. He listened and then commented, "Some people look for a sign from God to confirm His will; many devotees of St. Thérèse ask for a Rose"! It was good advice to give to a Carmelite, but that approach never appealed to me. Without any definite conclusion, I thanked him and told him I would continue to pray about it. Returning home from my encounter with Fr. Dare, I reflected on our conversation and wondered what I would consider a sign of God's will.

Carmelite House of Prayer, Oakville, California

Around this time of the year, I usually went to the races at Golden Gate Fields near San Francisco to celebrate St Patrick's Day with some Friars and secular Carmelite friends. It was a lovely day-out close to the San Francisco Bay, and it was great fun to see so many black, Afro-American ladies from the nearby city of Oakland, all dressed up in their green outfits and honoring St. Patrick with their shamrocks and green hats. At that time in 1994, my thoughts moved towards the feast of St. Patrick; I mused and laughed to myself: "If I get a good win at the races, that would surely be a sign for me"! But at the races, I was not doing too well discerning winners, and my funds were running low. On the second last race of the day, I invested the sum of $4.00 on a boxed exacta. I could hardly believe it when my two horses, "Trumpet Solo" and

"First Intent," came in first and second and paid off handsomely at $371.00.

I was flabbergasted, dumbfounded, and bowled over by the result. How could I deny or doubt that this big, excellent race win was 'my rose,' my sign from heaven?

3
Early Days in Uganda

"Sing to Him a new song"!

We return now to Uganda, where the three Carmelite missionaries, Bro. Bernard, Lillian Kelly, and I resided at the Bishop's house in Mityana. It was a gracious, loving introduction to the country – to be at the home of the Bishop and to enjoy his hospitality. One of the things that touched me was his way of pronouncing my name, David – it was the correct pronunciation, but it had a very distinctive tone that made me realize how happy he was that we had come to his Diocese. Later I noticed that the Vicar General, Msgr. Nkombya had a similar tone when he spoke to me personally. Both were good men. Both have passed on to their eternal reward. God rest their souls.

In Uganda, there are several different tribes, and within each tribe, many smaller groupings known as clans. This division can be confusing to the foreigner not only because of the other languages and dialects but also by being surprised that the black Ugandan man you try to communicate with is from a different part of the country and does not understand what you are saying! We can say that, in general, the people of Uganda are called the Baganda, but that is not correct. Although they are the largest group of people, the Baganda would only reach approximately 28% of the entire population. They are in the central and southern parts of Uganda, where our mission of Kyengeza is. The word for an individual Baganda is a Muganda, and the language of the Baganda is called Luganda. Are you confused? It takes time to figure out these differences. When we moved to Jinja, east of Kampala (see map on page 204), we were in Basoga territory, whose language is somewhat similar to that of the Baganda people. A little over two million people live in the Basoga territory, while the entire population of the country numbers approximately 30 million.

The three Carmelite missionaries: Bro. Bernard, Lillian Kelly, and Fr. David Costello.

Bishop Mukwaya is from the Baganda tribe and belongs to the "Buffalo" clan. He showed us some pictures of the buffalos and explained the connection with his family clan. He was inviting me to become a member of the Buffalo clan, which would be an honor and a cultural way of assuring me that I belong to his same family. It is another way of expressing welcome and hospitality, but at this juncture, I knew little about the clans and hesitated to enter some-thing alien to my own experience. I think he was disappointed, but I hope, not offended! Some years later, I met a native Ugandan Sister who was surprised I had not become identified with any tribe; she explained everything to me and installed me, without any formalities, as a member of the Buffalo clan. Moreover, she gave me a new name – "Kabugo" I think, but in truth, it has eluded my memory! One of our lay volunteers, Tim McCormack, made friends with a shopkeeper in Zigoti and got the name Nsereko as a new member of his friend's clan.

Bishop Mukaya's chauffeur, Brother Joseph, took good care of us and brought us to various places to meet members of the diocesan clergy, as well as to St. Kizito's parish, Kyengeza, destined to be our home for the coming years. However, Bishop Mukwaya decided to send us to the White Father's (Missionaries of Africa) parish at the far western side of the diocese, Kasambya, to learn the language and familiarize ourselves with the pastoral approaches of the diocese. The Pastor, Fr. Peter, a Dutchman, and his assistant pastor, Fr. Christian, a Belgian, warmly welcomed us. Fr Chris-tian, known by his nickname Kiki, was destined to be our Luganda teacher. A recently ordained native diocesan priest, Fr. John Paul Jumba, was the 3rd priest in residence at Kasambya. There was a clear and lovely spirit of co-operation and family among the priests and the staff. We felt at home right away. However, learning the language was not as easy as we hoped, but we persevered with Fr. Kiki's good-humored classes.

Lillian was learning the new language and already knew the essential prayers – the Our Father, the Hail Mary, and the Glory be. Bernard and I were not doing so well. Bernard got frustrated and depressed with the situation, and it burdened him. He talked about returning to the States and eventually followed through on that. He was a significant loss as he was the youngest and the strongest of the three of us; he was the one in whom many people placed great hopes.

My birthday is July 3rd, written in the USA as 7-3-36, which is read and understood differently in Africa and Europe as the 7th day of March. On that very day, someone who had discovered my 7-3-36 appendage prayed for me at the Prayers of the Faithful at Mass to wish me a happy birthday. Naturally, I did not correct the good parishioner in Church, but when we returned to the sacristy after Mass, I tried to inform my brother priests of the mistake. Fr. Kiki must have suspected the confusion because he hushed me immediately. "Don't say another word! Stay quiet! We will have two birthday celebrations for you this year"! It was an excellent excuse for ice cream and beer – if the same happened to be available!

I got malaria; I never got it in Kenya. Fr. Peter, a veteran of many years in Africa, recognized it right away and brought me to the local clinic for diagnosis and medication. Within a day, I felt better and soon returned to normal functioning. Lillian, the nurse, waved her finger at me, saying, "You did not take your 'Lariam' (malaria prevention medicine)"! Maybe I did miss it, but thanks be to God I recovered. I decided to enter the word LARIAM in big red letters in my calendar. That plan worked for a good while, but the mosquitos eventually grounded me again. Lariam is just one of the preventative medications for malaria. But it can have strong side effects, as Fr. Stephen experienced when he came to serve in our monastery in Jinja a few years later.

NEW BISHOP

During our time at Kasambya, Fr. Joseph A. Zziwa was nominated as the new Auxiliary Bishop of the Kiyinda-Mityana diocese. The Diocesan authorities arranged his consecration for March

16th. It brought great excitement to all in the diocese and the parish. Everyone wanted to attend the ceremony. Fr. Kiki arranged to bring Lillian, me, and a group of parishioners in his truck. But on the way, we were sideswiped by a big vehicle and pushed into the ditch.

Somehow Kiki was able to keep driving our truck and eventually got us out of the ditch. I was in the passenger seat, and when the big vehicle hit us on that side, my spontaneous prayer was "Jesus, Mary, and Joseph"! They were undoubtedly protecting us. As we struggled out, badly shaken, we saw the culprit vehicle disappearing down a side road. Thanks be to God no one was injured, and our truck escaped with only a few dents. Kiki decided we could continue our journey with caution and gratitude to God that no one was hurt and neither was there any significant damage to our truck. At the Mass for the consecration of the new Bishop, many priests concelebrated. During the handshake of peace, Kiki and I searched out one another to exchange greetings of peace and gratitude to God for our safety.

We persevered without Bernard, learning much from Peter, Kiki, and John Paul, three fine priests who became good friends. Bishop Mukwaya had sent us to Kasambya for three months. I figured the three months would end in mid-May, so I set my heart on going to Kyengeza by May 16th, the feast day of the great Carmelite saint who received the Scapular from Our Lady of Mount Carmel, Simon Stock.

Late in April, since no word was coming from the Bishop, I decided to go and see him personally and remind him of his promise. His curt response was, "You are not ready; you do not know the language; you stay longer at Kasambya." I tried to reason with him – "we will learn more at Kyengeza; you promised; we are getting tired of waiting." Nothing I said made an impression on the

Bishop, but I still had an ace up my sleeve – "Bishop, in honor of my 40th anniversary of ordination (April 29th), please let us go to Kyengeza." He paused for what seemed a long few minutes before coming out with a somewhat grudging "O.K." I was thrilled. Still, the Bishop reminded me of how missionaries did an exam in the native language before they took up their ministry. The exam, he said, would consist of him coming to confession to me to see if I understood him and how I would respond! When I shared this story with some local diocesan priests and asked them, "What kind of sins do Bishops commit"? We all had a good laugh. I remained apprehensive about my upcoming exam!

Bishop Zziwa with our missionaries and students. .

On May the 16th, the feast day of St. Simon Stock, Lillian and I arrived at our mission parish of St. Kizito, Kyengeza. We received a warm welcome by the Pastor, Fr. Kasimbi, the Associate Pastor, Fr. Matia Lutalo, the parish housekeeping staff, and many parishioners, or as they refer to them in Uganda – the Christians (just like the believers in Antioch as recounted in Acts 11:26). Eventually, the Pastor showed us our quarters; mine was "en suite" - it had a bedroom and bathroom but no running water! I had a bed and a table but no chair, no wardrobe, and a kerosene lamp to provide light. In Kasambya, our quarters had also been Spartan – simple guest rooms, outside toilets, and showers. Yet, we were happy to have arrived at our mission destination of St. Kizito's Rectory. Soon we realized that the Bishop's hesitance in allowing us to come to Kyengeza was his embarrassment at not providing us with a better set-up. It did not matter. It was a big house, even if the amenities were scarce. We also had simple guest rooms separate from the Rectory, where Lillian bunked down and where the kitchen staff had their rooms. We had come to live among the people, and we were happy.

Surprisingly, the most frustrating thing about our new situation was waiting for supper! The native priests liked to eat late, and even though the agreed-upon time for the main meal each evening was listed as 7.30 – 8.00 pm, nothing happened until around 9.00 pm. Then after the dinner, the two young lady cooks, Felicity and Harriet, joined us in the refectory for night prayers – and the Rosary on occasions – all in the Luganda language. However, the Ugandan food was tasty, healthy, and nicely presented. Since there was no refrigeration, we knew it was fresh and enjoyable. Celebrating Mass in the Luganda language was easy. It is a language written down by the colonists as they heard it spoken, but it was a different story to carry on a conversation. The greetings among the Baganda are formal and lengthy and not too demanding to remember. But after you cross that hurdle, a conversation becomes a big task for the newly arrived muzungus. Bishop Mukwaya advised us to talk with the children and "you will learn from them." I tried, but it did not work out that easily.

Andrew Bimpebwa

For the sermon, at Mass, I always looked out for someone who could translate my English, which for the most part, worked out well. But on occasions, I suspected the translator was wandering and going solo; some of the congregation also wondered; it was good fun to stop and question him and put him back on the right track. It recalled for me the Italian proverb – "Traduttore e tradittore" – the translator is a traitor. One of our best translators was a young Xaverian (a member of the Youth group to whom Lillian gave great attention), Andrew Bimpebwa. He became our first Carmelite Postulant and is now a solemnly professed member of the Jinja community.

NEW MISSIONARIES

Fr. Colm Stone, a native of Dublin, Ireland, and a long-time member of our Calif-Az region, responded to the call to mission in Uganda. His presence was a significant boost to our little community. We welcomed him with great joy, and he brought a new dimension to our house with his musical talents and good humor.

He would break into song at the evening meal, and we would join him to the best of our ability. He brought his tin whistle with him, and the melodic sounds that often wafted from his room gave entertainment and amusement to any visitors in our backyard. But perhaps, not to the roosters, who repeatedly pestered him at an early hour in the mornings, crowing their raucous greetings and disturbing his sleep. When that happened, Colm would advise the cook to "put that rooster in the pot" for supper! Colm was realistic about what he could do; he took good care of himself with his regular siesta and daily walks. He enjoyed meeting the "locals" on his afternoon strolls and especially communicating with the children in his limited Luganda and their broken English. In particular, he got great mileage from his encounter with a little one who spoke to him boldly and confidently with her hand out, saying, "Give - me - your - money"! Colm is also an accomplished clarinet player; I remember his excellent rendition of "Just a closer walk with Thee" at our parish folk Mass when we ministered together at St. Thérèse Parish in Alhambra, Los Angeles. Unfortunately, he did not bring his clarinet with him to Kyengeza.

One of Fr. Colm's priest friends was Fr. Dennis Kyemwa, Pastor of Our Lady of Mount Carmel parish of Busubizi, close to Mityana. Fr. Dennis was a good friend of all the Carmelites. He always sent his greetings to "the Stone"! That, of course, was Fr. Colm Stone. Fr. Dennis, a friendly and happy priest, held that we, as Carmelites, should have taken the parish of Our Lady of Mount Carmel. He claimed that he was willing to exchange his parish with us for Kyengeza parish! Fr. Dennis was the nephew of Fr. Karoli Lutwama, the well-known "First black, White Father," who in the 1940s offered to give Fr. Patrick Perjes OCD land to begin a Carmelite community of friars in Uganda.

Bishop Mukwaya told me how Fr. Karoli, although well

advanced in years, was still alive. Following through on this lead, I discovered he was in an Old Folks Home in Kampala, staffed by the Good Shepherd Sisters. I visited the home twice, the second time with Fr. Stephen, our Provincial. Fr. Karoli was very feeble and could not reply to our greetings and seemingly could not remember his meeting with Fr. Patrick Perjes. However, it was a joy to meet him, give him our blessings in his illness, and ask for his prayers on our efforts to begin a mission in Uganda. Fr. Karoli was due to celebrate his 100th birthday in December 2004. The actual date of his birthday was December 12th, but we planned to celebrate it after Christmas on December 29th.

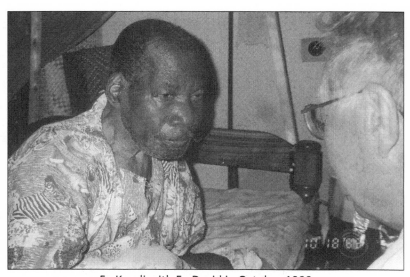

Fr. Karoli with Fr. David in October 1999

Fr. Dennis Kyemwa and I agreed to travel together to the special event. Unfortunately, Fr. Karoli died on December 18th, and we changed the funeral Mass to December 29th, the original date of the birthday celebration. We celebrated his life as a Missionary of Africa, gave thanks for his life of service to God and God's

44

people, and buried him in the cemetery attached to the Cathedral in Kampala. The Missionaries of Africa built the Cathedral, and on the front, it highlights the two great missionaries of Africa, Fr. Simeon Lourdel (Mapeera) and Bro. Amans. God rest all their souls.

Malaria is a common disease in Uganda, and many little children die. When afflicted, they can only cry and cry; their parents are too poor to buy the medication and often hope that it is a passing fever and put off looking for help until it is too late. Adults too fall prey to the same constraints of poverty and, when they feel a little better, do not complete the course but sell the remaining medication to someone else. Consequently, they are open to a new bout of the disease within a few weeks. No wonder the life expectancy in Uganda is just 48 years!

TWO CARMELITE SISTERS

Bishop Mukwaya told me with great joy about the coming of the active Carmelite Sisters from Austria. Before I could comment on this happy news, he added, "but you are not getting them at Kyengeza"! I innocently retorted, "why not, Bishop"? His reply was, "Kyengeza would have too many muzungus"! He told the Sisters to look around at the various parishes in the diocese and see which one they would like to choose; they did, and to our delight and his chagrin, they chose Kyengeza!

Sister Elizabeth (the Superior) and Sister Antonia came to join our community and took up residence in our guest rooms with Lillian and the female staff. Sr. Elizabeth immediately went to work in the kitchen, and soon she was serving delicious soups at our evening meals. Even after the Sisters built and moved to their new convent, delicious soups became a tradition for dinner. Sr. Antonia, a qualified nurse, began helping the many sick people and children who showed up at our doors. Lillian was also a nurse.

Sr. Elizabeth (in white), Sr. Antonia & Fr. Stephen, and two ladies (OCDS) in front of the Misigo Center in Mityana.

They worked well together and helped one another to understand the sick in their native language. Sr. Antonia quickly became the most proficient of all the missionaries in understanding and speaking the language and attributed this to the fact that she was repeating the same questions and answers to the sick. Her great love for the little ones was no doubt another way of learning the language.

Lillian felt very attracted to the youth group, the Xaverians, and was a great inspiration to them at Kyengeza. She also contacted the little group of Secular Carmelites, formed initially by the Nuns in Mityana, and got them to come to Kyengeza for their monthly meetings. Others from the parish became interested, figuring out what was distinct about being a lay Carmelite. One of our parishioners from the village of Mawundwe joined the group later. On one occasion, he thanked me profusely for having this monthly meeting of the Secular Carmelites on Sunday afternoons. Responding, I told him to thank Lillian. We priests were often at the out-stations for Masses on Sundays and did not return until around 5.00 pm. He continued, "If I did not have this meeting to come to, I would be at home with my friends in the village, sitting down with them and drinking the local brew"! Vincent sensed that there was more to life than hanging around, talking, and drinking beer. Later, Vincent's daughter joined the Carmelite Sisters, went to Austria for formation, and is now Sister Veronica, a professed community member at Kyengeza. The little Secular Carmelite community is flourishing and feels proud about belonging to the Carmelite family.

We settled in, gradually upgraded the living quarters, and protected the compound with a good fence around the Rectory area. The young native priests, Fr. Kasimbi and Fr. Matia, were always helpful, and we got along well together, as we also did with the young women who did the cooking and housekeeping. The people, and especially the children, were fascinated by the white men and women who came to live among them. For many of the children, our presence was the first time to see a white man or a white woman. When they saw us out for a good walk, some of them would jump up and down with shouts of "Muzungu! Muzungu!" but the smaller ones would run towards home crying out, "Mommie, Mommie! the white man is going to eat me"! It wasn't easy to get a good walk because many people would want us to stop and chat with them. We made many friends. We were happy to adjust to our new circumstances and get to know our people.

LEARNING THE LANGUAGE

Despite the encouragement of Bishop Mukwaya, and our poor

efforts to study and learn the local language, few of us made swift progress; it was a big struggle in the early years. At one stage, I felt like "giving up," as I compared myself with the European White Fathers and other missionaries in Kenya and Uganda. I wondered about the Lord's promise to his disciples "they will speak new languages"! I needed to deal with it and consulted with Bishop Zziwa, the new Auxiliary Bishop of the Diocese. He welcomed me, spoke to me kindly and encouragingly, and urged me to persevere. Later, at the clergy meetings, he arranged that there would be regular summaries in English after a discussion topic in Luganda. That was helpful, but it did not last too long! Fr. Colm attended these meetings with me, but when the discussion was all in Luganda, he would nudge me and ask for the truck's keys. He moved out and took a little nap! I felt obligated to remain in the hall.

Gradually, I felt more at ease and realized that the people often understood much more than I thought. The dependence on translators was good for our humility and allowing the Holy Spirit to work through our weaknesses.

4 Parish Leaders

"Don't walk ahead of me, I may not follow.
Don't walk behind me, I may not lead
Walk beside me and be my friend."

This anonymous verse speaks more of human interaction than leadership, but it does put a human face on a challenging task. It reminds us that we are all brothers and sisters. It echoes St. Teresa of Avila's advice to her sisters "in this house all must be loved, all must be held dear, all must be helped." Gospel leadership is more demanding in the sense that the leader must be the servant of all; and that the one who wishes to be first must sincerely seek to be the last. (Matthew 20. 26-28). Some leaders are anointed or selected because of their qualities and abilities; some are charismatic – outstanding in connecting to and inspiring the deepest longings of their people; others appear in the role of service, which is greatly appreciated and recognized.

THE SABUKRISTU
(*The Head Christian*)

Among the Christians (parishioners) of Kyengeza, Mark Gingo stood out as a genuine leader. He was on hand to warmly welcome us to Kyengeza and to accompany us to all the fourteen outlying sub-parishes. He spoke English well, was the accountant at the Mityana public hospital, and had a real place in the people's hearts for his sincerity and goodness. His wife, Rose, and their children were also highly esteemed by their fellow Christians.

Mark and Rose celebrate their Silver Jubilee

Mark had "run" for public office, and although he was not elected, that did not lessen the respect of his fellow Christians. Mark was not too worried about keeping time, which of course, is very understandable for a popular public figure who was always willing to greet and help others. Welcoming people is a crucial part of Uganda's culture. Greetings can be elaborate and lengthy. One time a policeman stopped me for a minor traffic infringement. I immediately defended myself; he gently put me in my place by simply noting, "you did not even greet me, sir"! the people expected you to ask, "How are you"? "How have you passed the day (or the night)"? "how is the family"? "is it peaceful in your locality"? All this and more before you get to the business on hand!

Later, Mark offered to present a seminar for the Catechists and other parish leaders. I was happy with his offer. It started late, at least one hour after the publicized time. I was intrigued to listen to Mark speaking with genuine competence and sincere acceptance by his audience, on guess what topic? --"Time Management"!

PARISH SECRETARY

Among the many fine Christians of Kyengeza parish, Godfrey Spire's presence at every parish gathering, as Parish Secretary, gives him the right to be listed as one of the parish leaders. He was not a personal secretary in the American sense of the word, but one who was present at all functions and ever ready to explain things competently. Godfrey also was a regular Lector at our parish Masses and an excellent translator of our English homilies. He was also the one who read out the notices after Holy Communion. Since there was no parish Newsletter or Bulletin, this part of the liturgy was necessary for the people. They wanted to question what was happening, give their own opinions, or ask for clarifications. Godfrey handled all these matters simply and directly, yet that part of the Mass could last for 30 minutes or even longer! We, muzungus, were often at a loss as to what was being discussed and had to endure it patiently, knowing that Godfrey was in charge and that it was for the good of the people.

Godfrey's father had donated the land for the original sub-parish of Kyengeza, which gave Godfrey a certain status among the people even if he was not as popular as Mark. He was tall, slender, stately, and somewhat mysterious, and from time to time, people wondered why he had such a prominent place at the liturgies and why he did not receive Holy Communion. His marriage situation was not regularized in the church, not even when we had a particular program for those who were just in civil marriages. One of Godfrey's sons worked for us a short while at the parish, and another one was a Postulant at Jinja for a brief period.

The donation of property to the Church can be a great blessing, but it can also come with unspoken expectations. It appears to be a "lease" or, as they say in Luganda, a "kibanja." Later, if the parish builds on it and is involved in some maintenance work, the donor or his family may claim remuneration. Buying or transferring property to a foreign person or group is legally complicated, as we discovered in Jinja in later years.

THE BWANAMUKULU

This Luganda word means the "big man." The Pastor often gets that title. I told my brother in Ireland –a pastor in various parishes – that the people called me the Bwanamukulu. He paused for a few moments before coming out with, "that would be a great name for a racehorse"!

The bwanamukulu did hire a personal assistant who could be considered the parish secretary. Her name was Prossy Nanfuka, and she took up residence in our guest quarters with Lillian and our two cooks and housekeepers, Felicity and Harriet, and later Olivia and Judith. They all got along well together and were good company for one another. Prossy was competent and discreet in dealing with the many people who came to the Rectory door looking for help. She was also available to help us with the language and translate our homilies into Luganda. (She and Judith were the ones who stayed with me in the hospital in Nsambya when I was seriously ill before returning to California).

THE CATECHISTS

Before we speak of individual catechists, it is essential to keep in mind the typical structure of a missionary parish. There is a central location for the main Church and Rectory (residence for priests), and then in a radius of approximately 10 to 30 miles, several sub-parishes or outstations. The sub-parishes are not easily accessible because of the poor roads, and lay Catechists are the local leaders. The catechists are well versed in their Catholic faith since most do a two-year intensive training course at the Catechetical Center. They work closely with the priests and are both a real blessing and genuine leaders among their people.

In our mission parish of St. Kizito, Kyengeza, the main Church and Rectory were close to the main road from Kampala to Mityana and Mubende. When we started the mission, the road from Kampala to Mityanda was full of potholes and dangerous. But strangely, the section from Mityana to Mubende was a good road. The people explained this difference by stating that Chinese workers who built the Kampala-Mityana section were more interested in catching snakes for their lunch. In contrast, the Yugoslavs workers who built the part from Mityana to Mubende did not relish snakes for their meal!

When we list the 15 sub-parishes of St. Kizito, the names sound like the words of the song "Those faraway places with strange-sounding names calling, calling, calling me home." Ddavula, Kabyuma, Kabule, Kamuli, Kiteete, Kito, Kysengeze, Magonga, Malangala, Mpirrigwa, Mugulu, Namungo, Tanda, Ttumba, and Kyengeza itself, which as well as being the name of the parish is also a sub-parish in its own right. They all have a catechist, and some have an assistant catechist, and most of them have their local Catholic Primary school. In his encyclical, Pope St John Paul II highlights the essential value of catechists in the Church.

"Among the laity...catechists have a place of honor... Churches that are flourishing today would not have been built up without them." (Redemptoris Missio).

Parish Catechists with their Retreat Master on left

The catechists came to Kyengeza each month for a regular meeting. They reported on the past month's activities and prepared for the next month. It was a friendly meeting, and when we built the Catechist's Hall, we had them very much in mind. We added some rooms where those who traveled a long distance could stay overnight. They were happy with that arrangement. Most came by bicycle or boda-boda – the small motorbike convenient and popular in Uganda. Whenever a catechist appeared during the week, someone in their sub-parish had died, and they were requesting a funeral Mass. I would ask "What time"? And would get the surprising answer "8 o'clock today" or maybe "3 o'clock tomorrow," indicating according to the Ugandan way of keeping time, this afternoon at 3 pm or tomorrow at 10 am. We made many mistakes with this method of time computation but gradually learned to be careful about our understanding of the scheduled event.

Refrigeration or funeral parlors were not available out in the country; burial had to occur soon as possible. The cemetery was a small section of the dead person's property. Sometime later, maybe a month or two or even longer, the "Last Funeral Rites" would be celebrated. The extended family were notified and would come for another Mass, choosing a successor to the deceased, and a family meal. It was a significant time of family gathering, friendship, reunion, and many times, even of reconciliation. At one of these last funeral rites, I discovered a curious type of "Baganda style Ecumenism." A Protestant minister member of the family sat beside me at the outdoor Mass in a friendly and respectful way. After the meal, when I went to the kitchen area to thank those who had prepared the meal, I discovered that they were Muslim family members. Some families encouraged intermarriage between Catholics and Protestants or Muslims, which hopefully would create a bond of peace and respect among themselves.

When we came to celebrate Mass at the sub-parishes, the catechists were always the first to welcome us. Then they would notify us how many baptisms we have at Mass, where would be the best place to have confessions, how many sick people need to be visited, and any other business that needed attention. There was always lots of singing at Mass. The offertory procession was always intriguing. The people brought up various gifts such as sugar cane, bananas, passion fruit, eggs, other vegetables, a chicken, and a few shillings: – all genuine expressions of their desire to give something of themselves to the Lord. The children came forward and seated themselves on the floor around the altar, from where they gazed with big eyes and great curiosity at the muzungu priest.

After Mass, some parishioners prepared a meal for the priest and the local dignitaries: – the catechist, the regional chairman, the school headmaster, and the homily translator. Then there would be visits to the sick on foot because often there was not even a semblance of a road to where the people lived. The catechist took care to load up the truck with the offertory gifts. We were happy to share, especially the sugar cane, that the children loved so much and were healthy for their teeth.

One of my first contacts with a catechist was in Mityana, where Fr. Colm and I were shopping. Some parishioners told Fr. Colm that the seriously ill Catechist from Kiteete was close to death and discharged from the hospital in Mityana but that his family had no way of bringing him back home. He had only a short time to live. Fr. Colm searched for me and our green Nissan truck and told me the story. He would need a vehicle to bring the Catechist and some of his relatives that were with him back home to die there. Fortunately, they had a mattress and arranged some form of a bed in the back of the truck. It must have been most uncomfortable and somewhat dangerous, but we still set out on our voyage of mercy. We moved slowly on the potholed road with the poor man and eventually reached his simple home in the sub-parish. The wife and the family were most grateful, and we were happy with our ministry to the dying man. He, too, was glad to get back home and died later that evening; God rest his soul. The next day we were back for the funeral Mass, and we had indeed learned a lesson about the precariousness of life in Uganda and the limitations of care for the poor.

That was not the first time I carried a dead or dying man in our trusty Nissan truck. The son of our head Catechist, Vincent, died in Mwera, and he had asked me to bring him back to the home place for burial. When I arrived, they had already wrapped him in the funeral clothing of bark cloth. The body was too long for the truck's bed, so we had to leave the tailgate open. I spontaneously gave a hand in getting him settled for the journey. It was a sad journey back to Vincent's home. Vincent thanked me over and over for what I had done and said, "you were not even afraid to touch the body"! It was only later that I found out that he had died of AIDS. Somehow the Lord gives us the grace to forget about the niceties of self-preservation in our ministry to the sick.

Vincent was the Head Catechist of our parish and one of the leaders in the diocesan organization of the Catechists. He was faithful, generous, and upright, and we became good friends. Another Catechist, Pafula Byekwaso, who was the Head Catechist of the parish, was also recognized by his peers in the diocese, who elected him Head Catechist for the Diocese. Not all our catechists were men. At Kyengeza, our catechist was Kevin Nagaddye. We also had Christine Nancha in Ddavula, Maria Nakato in Kito, and Dezirante Nayiga, an assistant in Magonga, all good people and faithful in their ministry. We always tried to show our appreciation for their work by providing them with water tanks and means of transportation, for which they showed their appreciation. The phrase in Luganda for "thank you" is "Weebale nnyo" or a more intense form "weebale nnyo, nnyo, nnyo" to which you might hear the response, "weebale kusima," which means "thank you for appreciating"! - all sincere expressions of a gracious people.

ANCESTORS IN THE FAITH

When we consider our living leaders in any area of life, we spontaneously go back in time to remember those who have expressed these same qualities in their own time. Mentioning our female Catechist from Kyengeza, Kevin Nagaddye calls to my mind a great missionary leader who has given her name to many females in Uganda and who is affectionally known as "Mama Kevina." In Uganda, we remember these great ancestors in the faith – the Ugandan Martyrs canonized by Pope Paul VI in 1964; the first missionaries to set foot on Ugandan soil, Missionaries of Africa (the White Fathers) Fr. Simeon Lourdel (known as Mapeera by the first Christians of Uganda) and his companion, Bro. Amans Delmas; and Mother Kevin, founder of two different religious communities of Sisters in Uganda. Their cause of beatification and eventual canonization is at its earliest stage, and hopefully, we will see them in the role of the Saints in the future.

Let me digress a little from the Mission of the Carmelites to briefly recall their lives and influence on the people of Uganda. The 22 Martyrs canonized by Pope Paul VI are at the very fabric of life in Uganda, among Catholics and Protestants. June 3rd of each year is a national holiday and feast day, celebrated with great solemnity at the National Shrine at Namugongo. At least one million pilgrims fill that shrine to honor those who gave their lives for the faith, including the youngest one, St. Kizito, who, when the leader St. Charles Lwanga hesitated to baptize him, replied, "too young to be baptized but not too young to die." Charles baptized him, and the fourteen-year-old Kizito died heroically for the faith rather than give way to the temptations of the King.

The two White Fathers, Mapeera and Brother Amans, landed at Kigungu, near Entebbe, in February 1879 and generously sowed the seed of the faith in Uganda. Their cause for canonization, together with that of Mother Kevin, was introduced in the Church in November 2016. They are now called "Servants of God." Before canonization, they will have to process through the cause of beatification. Let us pray that God will raise these three great missionaries in Uganda for His honor and glory and the good of the Church at large. I will focus a little more on Mother Kevin since our catechist of Kyengeza holds that name, and it is now a frequently used name among the women of Uganda (See map of Ireland on page 201).

Maria Teresa Kearney was born in 1875 into a relatively poor family at Knockanrahan, Arklow, County Wicklow in Ireland. Three months before Maria Teresa was born, her father died in an accident. Her mother remarried, but when Maria Teresa reached ten years of age, her mother too died, leaving a great void in the heart of this young Irish girl. She speaks of her mother in these words: "My mother introduced me into a spirituality of prayer and sound Catholic doctrine." A grandmother, Granny Grennell by name, then took care of her until tragedy once more came to the home with the grandmother's death. Maria Teresa was just seventeen. Like many poor Irish girls of her time, Maria Teresa made her way to London, where she got an assistant teacher's position and made acquaintance with the Franciscan Missionary Sisters. She joined their community at the age of twenty and two years later made her profession of vows. They gave her the name of Sr. Mary Kevin. It was not unusual for religious sisters to be given a male saint's name, and to have the name of Kevin for this Irish woman was unique in many ways.

St. Kevin was an austere hermit who lived in a cave on the banks of the lake in Glendalough, near where Maria Teresa grew up. Glendalough, the 'valley of the lake,' is a popular tourist attraction noted for its beauty and old monastic chapel. The youthful and vibrant Sr. Mary Kevin's dream was to go as a missionary to Baltimore or Virginia in the U.S.A., where her Sisters served the Afro-American people. God's plans for her were a little different as she got her assignment to begin a new mission, with five other Sisters, in Uganda. They reached their destination in 1902, almost exactly 100 years before the Carmelites arrived in Kyengeza. Their first home was in Kampala at Nsambya, and immediately they set out to meet the needs of the local people. Today Nsambya has a fine hospital and training center.

The Sisters responded generously to the needs of the local people and developed many practical ways of assisting them in the medical, educational, and religious areas of life. Gradually, Sr. Mary Kevin's leadership qualities came to the forefront, wonderfully expressing herself in the founding of two new Religious Congregations: - in 1923, the Congregation of the Little Sisters of St Francis and in1952, the Congregation of the Franciscan Missionary Sisters of Africa. She promoted her Sisters and African lay-women to ministries traditionally exclusive of women – midwives and doctors. Her influence spread to Kenya and Zambia. There are no fewer than an estimated 90 institutions and foundations related to her involvement and inspiration. She never lost her human and personal touch with the people of Uganda, fighting against ignorance, poverty, superstition, and witchcraft. She received the title of "Omugabi" (meaning the giver), from the people of Uganda, for her lavish generosity. During the second world war, she organized practical aid, gifts, and supplies for the Ugandan soldiers fighting in Burma. Emblazoned on the airplane that brought all these gifts was its name, "The Mama Kevina." Our Carmelite priest, Fr Patrick Perjes, was a prisoner of war in Uganda. Mother Kevin asked him to preach a retreat to her postulants preparing for their profession in the Mother House at Nkokengero. He also benefited from her generosity, with the gift of a Norton motorbike. It is no wonder that Ugandan mothers are delighted to name their new-born daughters in honor of this great missionary.

At 80 years of age, Mama Kevina headed off for the U.S.A. to raise funds for her many mission projects. There she met her great friend and benefactor, Cardinal Cushing of Boston, but she died peacefully in Boston, after a short illness, in 1955. The sisters of her community brought back her body to Ireland for burial. Still, the cries of the Uganda people prevailed so that her remains were eventually sent home to Uganda for her final resting place at the Motherhouse in Uganda, Nkokengero, not far from our own House of Formation, "Duruelo" in Jinja.

Mother Kevin's cause for beatification, with Fr. Simeon Lourdel (Mapeera) and Brother Aman, was formally introduced in 2016. We now call them "Servants of God" and look forward to the day when they will be named among the Saints of the church and join the Ugandan Martyrs as truly "Our Ancestors in the Faith." We, Carmelites, are privileged to walk in their shadow and follow somehow in their footsteps.

Icon depicting Carmellite saints, Ugandan martyrs, and local Christians under the protection of our Blessed Lady (Virginia Barber OCDS)

5
Discalced Carmelite Family

"The hills are alive with the sound of music..."

The Discalced Carmelite family consists not just of the Friars – male members, priests, and brothers. It includes the Nuns - enclosed religious women; the Sisters - several active religious congregations who claim the Spirit of Carmel and live out its charism in an apostolic setting and the Secular Order – lay men and women who follow the universal call to holiness in the lay state. As well as the Friars at Kyengeza and Jinja, there is also a monastery of enclosed contemplative Nuns at Kiyinda, Mityana, and the congregation of Sisters of Mary of Mount Carmel, serving at Kyengeza and Misigo in the Mityana diocese. The Secular Carmelite communities usually spring up where there is already a presence of the Nuns or Friars, under whose guidance they flourish.

THE NUNS
The history of the Carmelite Nuns of Kiyinda, Mityana, goes back to the days of the Second Vatican Council when two Arch-

bishops, one from Kampala and the other from Augsburg, Germany, struck up a friendship in Rome. Archbishop Kiwanuka of Kampala and Archbishop Stimpfle of Augsburg talked about the missionary activity of the Church. At that time, the diocese of Kiyinda-Mityana as such was not yet in existence – it became a diocese in 1981 – but they focused on Mityana, the site of the local Ugandan Martyrs (Noe Mawaggali, Luka Bannakintu, and Matia Mulumba), as an appropriate location to begin a new mission. Fr. Henry Eudenbach and some other priests came to explore that possibility in Mityana. At the same time in Germany, the missionary spark touched the flourishing monastery of the Carmelite nuns of Welden. They had twenty-one nuns in that community, so thoughts moved spontaneously to a possible new foundation. Twelve of the twenty-one nuns volunteered to go to Africa, and finally, eight made up the team for this new missionary venture. Eventually, these brave religious set out with a few lay helpers for Uganda.

Mityana nuns

They were warmly welcomed by priests and people, even though the idea of an enclosed religious community was alien to the Ugandan thinking and experience. At this stage, they were only familiar with active religious sisters. The native priests wanted the Nuns to accompany them on their ministry in the sub-parishes. The laypeople looked to the white Sisters from Germany for material help. Many came knocking at their doors at all hours, looking for help. "Enclosure" was indeed a foreign concept, but the Nuns learned and adapted. Gradually they got their monastery set up and formed a lay group called HOSFA (hope sharing family) to supervise their good works. The new monastery includes a small section outside the cloister, where priests and people might come for private retreats. Other HOSFA activities, sponsored by the nuns, saw the establishment of a small medical clinic that has now developed into the fine hospital of St. Francis in the town of Mityana. Other projects such as a Vocational school, a Carpentry shop in Zigoti, and a small farm, were practical ways of assisting young people. They also constructed an enclosed monastery suitable for their contemplative lifestyle.

Yet, all this growth was not without severe outside problems. The years of Idi Amin's rule, with its wars and violence, had a devastating effect on everyone's life. Many people fled from the soldiers and sought refuge in the monastery for safety and survival. At one time, over 80 people took shelter in the monastery's sanctuary, and the sisters had to confront the armed soldiers who came in search of so-called enemies of the ruling regime. The soldiers were confronted courageously by the nuns who asked them to lower their rifles and respect the sacredness of the monastery. The soldiers did so. But everything was not resolved that easily; four of the nuns were convicted and expelled from the country for not having up-to-date work permits – hardly a serious crime. They went into exile in the nearby region of Kenya, where they received welcome and hospitality from the nuns of the Nairobi and Tindinyo Carmels. All the community remained steadfast in their commitment to the mission in Uganda – valiant women for sure.

Gradually vocations appeared, and on the Golden Jubilee of the monastery's foundation in 2017, they elected as Prioress a native Ugandan, Sister Mary Helen. She was not the first Ugandan Prioress; that honor goes to Sister Mary Grace from Ttumbu, an out-station of the Kyengeza parish. In our earlier days at Kyengeza, we prayed the Divine Office on the house veranda, looking up at Ttumbu in the distance. That little Church held a great fascination and a great inspiration for us; it was a joy for us to go there for Mass and meet Sr. Grace's parents and family members. We knew that a Carmelite nun at Kiyinda monastery had a personal love and fervent prayers for her native parish, now staffed by her Carmelite brothers. Ttumbu was a good climb on foot and became a favorite place for a Saturday morning hike by Lillian. It was good exercise; Lillian knew all the shortcuts.

The Nuns' dedication and prayer life are a great blessing to the local Church and the whole Church. Their presence at Kiyinda, Mityana, is a huge blessing for the Diocese. At the same time, we found inspiration and support from their joyful commitment to the Carmelite ideals and enjoyed a gracious welcome whenever we visited the monastery. It was a joy to be greeted by the smiling out-sister, Sister Ulrike, and experience the goodness and hospitality of the community.

THE ACTIVE SISTERS

We have already described the coming of the Sisters of Our Lady of Mount Carmel to Uganda, and their selection of the parish of St Kizito, Kyengeza, as their preferred place of ministry. This

Carmelite congregation came into existence in Linz, located in the northwest of Austria, in 1861.

They were, originally, a group of OCDS (Secular Carmelites) who longed to live an enclosed community life as Carmelite Nuns. The local Bishop, Franz-Joseph Rudigier, directed them to more urgent needs in his diocese. This social and charitable work became their apostolate as Carmelites. They developed well in Austria and Germany in the tradition of Carmel, inspired by the prophet Elijah and the great Carmelite teachers of prayer, Teresa of Avila and John of the Cross.

The first two Sisters to arrive at Kyengeza were Sr. Elizabeth and Sr. Antonia. They had to learn two new languages, English and Luganda. They spent some time in London to learn English before coming to Africa. Sr. Antonia is French-born and learned German when she went to Austria before joining the community there. She has a natural talent for languages but sometimes provided us with amusement and confusion as she moved, unaware of it herself, from English to Luganda and into German. The gift of tongues is undoubtedly a blessing but of little use unless the hearers have the gift of understanding. Sr. Elizabeth, coming from a farming family, showed many talents in cooking, organizing, teaching, and supervising the building of their new convent at Kyengeza. She used her farming gifts in developing their property for crops and animals. Bishop Mukwaya had told us to give the Sisters ten acres of the parish land. Most of that was "bush," but with the help of many willing parishioners, we were able to clear it for the foundations of their new convent. It was a great day of celebration when Bishop Zziwa blessed the new convent in 2003. Interestingly, the architect and the builder, both missionary priests, were from the Hoima Construction Company, a group formed and directed by the White Fathers. It is a fine, elegant building, admired and appreciated by all the neighbors.

Sr. Antonia, born in France, entered the community in Austria where she got to know and admire them when working as an "au pair" in the lovely land of the "Sound of Music."

A qualified nurse, she renewed her license for functioning in Uganda, and in that capacity, helped many sick people in the parish. Her love for the little ones and music attracted many to the convent. She formed a little group of children called the "Ebimuli" (The Flowers) and, as a choir, sang at Sunday Masses and grew in love for their heavenly patron, the Little Flower, St Thérèse. Since the children and people of Uganda love to sing and dance, the lovely rolling hills of their country soon came alive with the sound of music directed by our French sister. Sr. Antonia was efficient and helpful in developing our mission's SACC (Sponsor A Child, Carmelite) program. She also worked closely with us and was a great inspiration for the building of the Little Flower School. Continuing her practical bent and awareness of the needs of the little ones, she established a particular home for the sick and handicapped from the Little Flower School and for those she discovered on her parish visitation. In Uganda, as in many places worldwide, people are often ashamed of the handicapped members of the family and try to conceal them from the public. Sr. Antonia was alert to this reality and helped many to grow and become loved and treasured as children of God.

The sisters of Mary of Mount Carmel

Soon Sr. Edith and Sr. Margret joined the two foundresses and added further variety to our parish ministry. As the oldest of the four sisters, Sr Margret got the name "Sr. Jaja." Jaja is the Luganda word for grandmother or grandfather and is applied frequently to older people. Sr. Margret has a great love for the elderly poor and moved about the parish with serenity and peace that no one could disturb. Sr. Edith, as well as keeping everything in order in the convent, is a talented singer and soon joined the Parish choir donning the colorful choir robes over her Carmelite brown habit. As well as being a hairdresser for her sisters, she often gave Fr. Colm or me a good haircut on the Rectory veranda. I had tried to get a haircut in three of the local barbershops in Zigoti. They just refused to attempt dealing with this new foreign customer. Eventually, one claimed to be competent, but it was an ordeal for the barber to satisfy the muzungu's hairstyle directives and spontaneously attracted a crowd to watch this unusual event in the Zigoti barbershop!

What a blessing to have Sr. Edith and her Carmelite sisters to work with us at our mission parish, and what a joy to share with them our Carmelite spirit in the service of God's people. Thanks be to God they have attracted native vocations who will carry on their excellent work

OCDS

The OCDS or Secular Carmelites are the 3rd group in the immediate Carmelite family. They are not simply loosely affiliated with the Order because of their name or their liking for the Carmelite spirituality. They are a juridical part of the Order and consequently follow both the laws of the Church and the Carmelite-approved legislation. In the past, it was common to have a "Confraternity of Our Lady of Mount Carmel" in Carmelite Churches whose members participated in Carmelite devotions and often did some service in the local Church. At that time, the name used for a greater connection with the parent Order was the "Third Order." The Secular Carmelites are more structured with their regulations and find inspiration from the same Rule of Life - the Rule of St. Albert of Jerusalem - that the Nuns and Friars follow. They strive to live in the context of their lay status, the "universal call to holiness" which the Second Vatican Council documents propose. The Council, in turn, received inspiration from the teaching and example of St Thérèse of Lisieux, now a Doctor of the Church. She presented her style of holiness - the Little Way - as open to everyone, even "little souls" like herself.

In recent years, the OCDS has been experiencing remarkable growth in numbers worldwide, even as the Nuns and Friars are struggling with a lack of vocations. They are indeed a "sign of the times" as they take greater responsibility for the life of the Church. Some religious orders or congregations have developed a noticeably clear relationship with their lay associates, for example, in the medical field of "Carondolet Health" and education of "LaSallian Schools." The Christian Brothers cultivate the spirit of their founder, St. John Baptist De La Salle, with special training for their school staff in his quality and style of education. However, they may have little direct or immediate responsibility in their schools.

We, Carmelites, are still at a tentative level of this new reality. But in our Uganda venture, we have an outstanding example in Lillian Kelly, OCDS, who was a founding member of the mission. She served generously and efficiently in developing a local OCDS group and as the director of health services in the diocese. The OCDS members rallied to support the mission in many other ways – by prayer, recycling projects, financial help, sponsorship of needy children (SACC), and the Pilgrimages to Uganda. There is still much more that they can do with creative leadership and trust in God for whom "nothing is impossible."

RELATED COMMENTS

As is his duty, the local Bishop observes what is happening and how things develop among the missionaries. Sometimes he discovers talents that he could use efficiently in the more extensive diocesan needs. He will then request the community's Superior to allow the competent person to serve at the Diocesan level. How can the

Superior refuse? We have already told the story of our mission volunteer, Lillian Kelly, called to serve as Diocesan Health Director. Then Bishop Zziwa asked Sr. Elizabeth to supervise the already established Diocesan Retreat and Conference Center at Misigo in Mityana and requested Sr. Antonia to be the "Focal Person" for AIDS ministry in the Diocese. Both accepted and adapted to their new situations. Sr. Elizabeth had to move residence to the Misigo center, and Sr. Margret accompanied her. Sr. Antonia remained at Kyengeza and worked from there, as Lillian did, with her diocesan duties. The Misigo venture has grown into a second foundation for the Sisters. Sr. Antonia also did her AIDS ministry with enthusiasm and effectiveness, but severe health issues forced her to withdraw from the AIDS work and focus on her duties at Kyengeza. Thanks be to God she recovered well and continues her missionary presence from Kyengeza.

INDIVIDUAL FRIARS

Among the Friars, individuals are assigned to the mission for the most part on a volunteer basis. It also happens that an individual friar may be recommended for the mission by another authority outside the Province. When Fr. Stephen Watson served on the General Council in Rome, Fr Zdenko Krizic from Croatia, the Vicar General, and the First Councillor frequently talked together about their Provinces. Fr Zdenko suggested that one of the Croatian Friars, Fr. Anto Stepanovich, might do well in the mission even though he was a little "unsettled" in the home region. Fr. Stephen passed the word on to the Calif-Az province. Everyone was happy with this new missionary recruit. Fr. Anto came to California to study English and eventually reached Kyengeza with high expectations from himself and the community. But loads of goodwill and enthusiasm are no guarantee of a missionary vocation. He did not fit in and moved to Malawi for a further trial with similar results. Back home in Croatia, he took a leave of absence from his Carmelite community and served in a Diocesan parish. God bless and guide him.

Fr. Edmond Shabani OCD, from the Democratic Republic of the Congo, was recommended for our mission by Fr. Zacharie Igirukwayo, a native of Burundi and the assigned General Councillor for Africa. I knew Edmond from my days in Nairobi and welcomed him to Kyengeza. There was no problem with the language, as Fr. Edmond picked up Luganda quickly, just as he had learned English easily in Nairobi. He served well for the first few years and even took on the responsibility of Postulant Director of the first group in the rented house in Jinja.

When I became ill and had to return to California, Bishop Zziwa requested that Fr. Edmond take over as Pastor at Kyengeza. That led to a shuffle of personnel, but Fr. Edmond, well-liked by the Bishop, did well at Kyengeza. Fr. Larry Daniels had also been with us at Kyengeza and had formation experience from Nairobi, so he became the Postulant Director. All went well until some accusations against Fr. Edmond led to the General Councillor from Africa, Fr. George Tambala, coming to make a formal Visitation of the mission. The result was that Fr. Edmond was sent back to the Congo. I was convalescing in California at that time. I received an email from Fr Edmond, stating somewhat cryptically that the General Councillor was sending him back to the Congo "for farther (sic) studies." That left Kyengeza and Jinja in great need that we will speak about later.

Such are the uncertainties of the mission situation. We are all weak and vulnerable human beings called to serve the Lord and His people. Not long after Fr. Edmond returned to the Congo, the friars of that region elected him to their Provincial Council, and after that term, he went to Nigeria for further studies. May the Lord bless him and guide him.

Fr. Larry Daniels had been my Superior at the House of Studies in Nairobi and served there for many years. When he had to return to his Washington Province after his assigned term, with many health issues and, despite the concern of his Superiors, he had such a great love for Africa he wanted to return. His Superiors did not support him in this desire. On a visit to Africa, he and Fr. Dennis Geng came to Kyengeza to see me and explore the possibility of Fr. Larry coming to Kyengeza. I was happy to welcome him, and when he

Fr. Larry Daniels

came, it was a blessing for our mission parish. It became a further blessing when Fr. Edmond returned to the Congo since Fr Larry was competent to take on the position of Postulant Director at Jinja. He continued in that role until we opened our own house in Jinja, and he remained with us until Fr. Stephen was assigned to the Jinja House and became the Formation Director. After Fr. Stephen was settled, Fr. Larry applied to return to Nairobi. He proved his worth and went back to serve in the land and among the people he loved so much. He is now the Superior of their new Retreat House in the Ngong Hills near Nairobi. Thank you, Fr. Larry.

6
CHARISM and CULTURE

"Don't fence me in"

In the years that followed the conclusion of the Second Vatican Council, several difficult situations surfaced in the Catholic Church. Perhaps the most critical one was the birth-control issue, which the Holy Father, Pope St. Paul VI, tried to resolve by his famous "Humanae Vitae" letter. Another concern was the decline in devotion to the Blessed Virgin Mary. The Holy Father dealt with that competently in his Apostolic Letter, "Marialis Cultus." Another problem was the missionary activity of the Church. For this, his encyclical "Evangelii Nuntiandi," or in its English title "On Evangelization in the Modern World," was written in 1975 and is highly esteemed by our present Holy Father, Pope Francis. Fr John Hurley's C.S.P. (Consultant and Missionary for New Evangelization Strategies) comment on that Encyclical stated: "it has been and continues to be the impetus for getting out of our comfort zone." These words summarize the attitude that was developing after the Vatican Council years. The changes in theology, liturgy, and pastoral approaches left many with an inward focus and forgetful of the foreign missions. The fall-off in vocations to the priesthood and religious life compounded this problem. There was a tendency to leave the foreign missionary activity of the Church to the traditional missionary congregations, such as the Missionaries of Africa ("The White Fathers"), the Verona Fathers ("Combonis"), the Spiritans, ("Holy Ghost Fathers"), the Maryknoll Congregation, and other new congregations springing up in Africa – the Apostles of Jesus, and the Guadalupe Missionary community from Mexico.

In that context that Pope Paul called on the traditional religious Orders – the Franciscans, the Dominicans, the Augustinians, the Carmelites, the Trappists - "Go to Africa and enrich the Church there with your charism." This rallying cry of the Holy Father challenged the somewhat simple missionary philosophy expressed in the brief statement: "Get in, get on and get out." The old missionary style was to go to the assigned territory, build up the Church with great dedication and sacrifice, and then move on to a new location. Missionaries developed parishes and schools, cultivated vocations for the local diocese, often set up and staffed seminaries, and then handed them over to the diocese. Pope Paul VI felt that many dioceses in mission lands were missing out on the unique gifts that religious orders could bring, which would enrich the Church in these new missionary places.

Pope Paul VI, when he visited Uganda for the canonization of the Ugandan Martyrs in 1964 and then on a second occasion in 1969, observed the wealth of vocations in that country. As the Universal Pastor, he did not hesitate to urge them to become missionaries to their brothers and sisters of their continent. The Church must reach out to the ends of the earth in the spirit of the command Jesus gave us before He ascended into heaven. The Diocese of Mityana did not fail to answer this call of the Holy Father. One of the Diocesan priests who served at Kyengeza, Fr. Charles Matumbwe, was a "Fidei Donum" (gift of the faith) missionary priest in South Africa, where he learned the clicking language of the Xhosa people. However, in the western world, we are more familiar with the significant number of African or Indian priests who come to serve here in the U.S.A. They come to help in the context of our lack of native vocations and for their economic reasons. There is the concern – why are so many foreign priests and religious coming here, and why do our communities set up Mission areas in foreign lands simultaneously? To try to answer these questions would take up a lot of space and time that would stray from the goal of these memoirs, but they do need to be examined thoroughly and thoughtfully in the spirit of the Gospel.

CARMELITE CHARISM

The Carmelite Charism is often expressed succinctly as the "way of contemplative prayer." That does not mean that every Carmelite is a contemplative. Still, it does indicate that they have a good knowledge of the growth of the prayerful relationship with God. They express it as an enclosed lifestyle (the nuns), an appreciation of silence, and a ministry with an accent on interior prayer (friars, active sisters, and secular Carmelites). Contemplation is a freely given grace – the Living Water - promised to the Samaritan woman in John's Gospel, chapter 4. When accepted, it gradually transforms the soul and sets it on fire with the generous service of the Church and God's people. St. John of the Cross defines contemplation as "a secret, peaceful and loving inflow of God in the soul, which, if not hampered, can set the heart on fire with love" (Dark Night of the Soul, Bk. 1, Ch. 10, par 6; *The Collected Works of St John of the Cross*, translated by Kieran Kavanagh OCD and Otilio Rodriguez OCD, ICS Publications, 2131 Lincoln Rd. NE, Washington, D.C. 20002-1199).

St. Teresa of Avila, the foundress of the Discalced Carmelites, was fascinated, even from her childhood, by the story of the Samaritan woman in John's Gospel, chapter 4, 5-42. She also dearly loved the words of Jesus at the Feast of Tabernacles, in the same Gospel of John, chapter 7, 37-39.

> On the last and greatest day of the feast, Jesus stood up and exclaimed, "Let anyone who thirsts come to me and drink. Whoever believes in me, as scripture says:
>
> 'Rivers of living water will flow from within him.'"
>
> He said this in reference to the Spirit that those who came to believe in him were to receive.

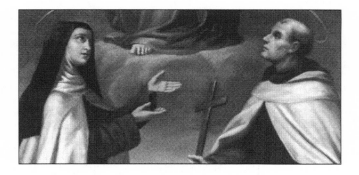

These words, according to Teresa, clearly indicate the Lord's strong invitation of everyone to receive the Living Water of contemplation, the gift of the Spirit.

Teresa describes the growth in prayer with the image of Watering a Garden in four progressively easier stages – a) using buckets to draw water, b) getting the water using a waterwheel, c) clearing a channel from the source, and d) an abundant rain. Her classic, the "Interior Castle," focuses on the awareness of God's presence in the depths of the soul and the transformation through God's action. (*The Collected Works of St Teresa of Avila*, translated by Kieran Kavanagh OCD and Otilio Rodriquez OCD, ICS Publications.)

Likewise, St. John of the Cross, her companion in the Reform of the friars, outlines the growth of the spiritual life, through darkness and light, to the grace of transforming union. Both these great Carmelites are Doctors of the Church, and we know that their teaching is for the benefit of God's people. They are 'Mystical Doctors' because they include the extraordinary experiences of God's dealings with individual Christians on the journey of prayer.

St. Thérèse of the Child Jesus, a Doctor of the Church, follows a more ordinary way – the Little Way – to reach the same transforming union with God. Thérèse's experiences of God are not "mystical" but ordinary, and as such, have a great popular appeal. (*Story of a Soul: The Autobiography of St. Therese of Lisieux* by John Clarke OCD, ICS Publications, Washington D.C.)

These three Carmelite teachers explore their relationships with God based on their own unique experiences in life. For example, the presence of God within the soul, even the soul in the state of mortal sin (Teresa), the presence of God in poverty and the harsh, unjust prison experience suffered in a Toledo jail (John), the hidden longings and dreams – even the desire to be a priest – in the depths of her soul (Thérèse).

Every one of us has experiences of God in our lives, but not everyone follows through with them in prayer. In the African setting, we might think of Josephine Bakhita, the little Sudanese girl of about nine years, who thought of a higher Being by looking up at the night sky. She wondered: "Who made all these wonderful things; who is Master of the stars and the moon"? That was before she knew anything about Christianity. This natural contemplation enabled her to recognize the Creator, then come to the knowledge of the Savior, and eventually become a canonized saint. On a different level, the young Martyrs of Uganda willingly accepted the verdict of death by fire rather than give in to the immoral demands of the King. The Head catechist, Charles Lwanga, was very hesitant to baptize the young Kizito, knowing that he would also have to die. Little Kizito of fourteen years of age replied with great courage, "too young to be baptized, but not too young to die," and so he joined the group of twenty-two and was burned alive at the rage of the King. Not everyone will have the courage and witness of the Ugandan Martyrs. But every Christian's destiny is the call to intimacy with God in prayer and to partake of the Living Water promised by Jesus.

Sometimes we claim that such heights of spirituality are beyond the capacity of everyday people or even ordinary priests. Yet, the great missionary of Germany, St Boniface, reminds us,

"Let us preach the whole of God's plan to the powerful and the humble, to rich and poor, to men and women of every rank and age, as far as God gives us the strength, in season and out." (*The Liturgy of the Hours*, Volume II, page 1865, Catholic Book Publishing Co. New York, 1976.)

Often, the contemplative life is not understood, as was the case of the Carmelite Nuns when they first came to Mityana. The people had no offense in mind; they simply had no experience of enclosed religious communities. Others question the value of "all this praying" because there is so much pastoral work to be done. Even among our Carmelite students in Nairobi, as I tried to instill in them the priority of prayer over a football game, there was friction and defensiveness on both sides. But we remember Teresa received criticism for preparing chicken in place of the regular austere fish diet. Her reply, "there is a time for penance and a time for partridge," shows her broad-mindedness and true freedom of spirit in following the strict requirements of the enclosed nuns.

In my preaching in the parish at Kyengeza, I liked to include the words of Jesus given to us in John's Gospel chapter 10, verse 10, "I came so that they might have life and have it more abundantly." I was not promoting a contemplative way of life but somewhat aware of the people's poverty, that the Lord wanted to bless them generously. There was never any questioning of my use of this text, but at one of our monthly catechists' meetings as I elaborated a little on it, I was stopped in my tracks when one of the catechists interrupted me with the question … "Then Fr., why are we poor"? That was a sincere effort to make sense out of the words of Jesus in the context of poverty. Stumbling to explain, I became keenly aware of the need to see and explain the beauty of the Gospel and the promises of Jesus from the listeners' perspective.

It makes little sense to call to mind the promise of the "Living Water" of intimacy with God in prayer when people need to carry heavy jerry cans of polluted water home that they must boil before drinking it. Clean water is a basic human need but not readily available in developing countries. We need to preach the Gospel and the Carmelite charism in the context and the realities of poverty. Clean water became a big part of our ministry, which we will deal with in the next chapter on Human Development.

RAHNER AND THE FUTURE

Before I conclude this chapter, I would like to share an experience from my final year of ministry in Kenya. Teaching Spirituality at the college in Tangaza meant that we put on an annual symposium of public presentations related to current events. In 1999 the overall topic was "Paradigms of Spirituality for the New Millennium." As in every nation, there were great hopes in Africa as 2000 drew near. My assigned topic was "Christians of the Future." It came from the frequently used phrase of the great German theologian Karl Rahner, S.J.- "The Christian of the future will be a mystic, or he will not exist at all." (confer. Rahner, S.J., Karl, *Theological Investigations*, London: Daron, Longman & Todd 1981. Vol XX, Concern for the Church, page 149).

It was an absolute joy to investigate this theologian's writings and see how thoroughly and carefully he presented his case. It is undoubtedly not some sudden or passing insight but a well-thought-out and intelligent analysis of what is happening in the Church and the world. No wonder he is considered one of the great theologians of the last century, imbued with a great love for the Church in his role as a true theologian.

He outlines five characteristics of the Spirituality of the Church, and it is in dealing with the 3rd one that he makes the statement about the Christian of the future. Let me try to summarize the five characteristics of God's dealings with us human beings:

1) Continuity with the past, the entire Salvation history. This respect for the past also includes openness to the Spirit, who leads us to new forms of expression.

2) The essentials of the Christian faith; Jesus, the authentic model of humanity, and Mary, the model of womanhood.

3) We will be Christian only by personal discovery, that is, by conviction and dedication; we will not be carried along by any public acceptance or recognition. This conviction and commitment can only be sustained by the "solitary, immediate *experience* of God and his Spirit," not by doctrinal teaching, rational arguments, or public approval. Rahner is careful to point out that he is not referring to extraordinary mystical phenomena but *the ordinary, down-to-earth experience of God's presence and action in our lives.*

4) Highlights the aspect of community. This community quality balances off the previous intensely, individualistic one: "the solitary experience of God." Here he is not talking about a loose grouping of people but, as he puts it, "a communal experience of the Spirit." That is present in the Church today through the renewal of the Liturgy, the Charismatic movement, and small Christian community groups. The advances in communication skills and group dynamics can enhance the functioning of groups and can aid our Christian longing for genuine community.

5) A humble attachment and fidelity to the Church that would be open to the mystery of God's presence and power working through human weakness.

Rahner ends his commentary on the "Spirituality of the Church of the Future" with the following personal reflection:

"Allowing for all reservations about the unforseeability of the concrete shape of future Catholic spirituality, have I succeeded in naming some few perhaps arbitrarily selected particular characteristics of this spirituality? I can't be certain, but may I hope so"?

OTHER VOICES

Many other writers have considered the future of the Church and its spirituality. Not all of those I present come from an African viewpoint, and they may clarify our attempt at linking culture and charism in Kenya and Uganda. They also would loosely correspond to the five characteristics of Rahner mentioned above.

1) Donal Dorr, an Irish missionary and theologian of the St Patrick's Kiltegan Missionary Society, has worked in Africa and Latin America. His main contention is that we need to integrate Spirituality and Justice. For this balanced spirituality, he frequently uses the famous text of Micah 6. 8:

"You have been told, O man, what is good, and what the Lord requires of you: Only to do the right and to love goodness, and to walk humbly with your God."

This text surely situates our current longings in continuity with the Old Testament longing for justice. (Also confer *Integral Spirituality*, 1990, Orbis Books, Maryknoll, New York 10545, and *Spirituality and Justice*, published in Ireland by Gill and MacMillan, Dublin 8.)

2) John Waliggo is a well-respected Ugandan theologian and has written about the flourishing area of African Christology: Who is Jesus for the people of Africa? What image of Jesus makes sense for Africa? Jesus as Healer, as Ancestor and Elder Brother, as Chief and as Liberator all have a particular attraction, but Waliggo chose the image of "Jesus,

84

the Suffering Servant" in *The Faces of Jesus in Africa* (Robert J.Schreiter, editor).

Fr. John Walligo

It is a little surprising that this Ugandan native did not choose the "Martyrs of Uganda" whose memory dominates the Church in Uganda and whose names and personal witnesses are celebrated and invoked by the Christians. They name their Churches, schools, parishes, and sub-parishes in memory of the Martyrs. Their National holiday on June 3rd always draws a vast gathering of approximately one million pilgrims to the Martyrs' shrine at Namugongo.

3) Carlo Carretto is an Italian "Little Brother of Jesus" and writes from his base and experience in the Sahara, *Letters from the Desert* (William Collins Inc., 1979, New York). He had been active in Catholic Action in Italy but moved to the desert in response to an inner voice "Leave everything, come with me into the desert. I don't want your action any longer. I want your prayer, your love." He also ministered in Hong Kong, from where he wrote *The Desert in the City*.

Carretto links contemplation and poverty in his challenging spirituality, "Contemplation in the streets; this is tomorrow's task not only for the Little Brothers but for all the poor." His advice on practicing a genuine contemplative way of life is clear and demanding,

> "One hour a day, one day a month, eight days a year, for longer if necessary, you must leave everything and everybody and retire alone with God. If you don't look for solitude, if you don't love it, you won't achieve contemplative prayer. If you can do so, but nevertheless, if you do not withdraw to enjoy intimacy with God, the fundamental element of the relationship with the All-Powerful God is lacking - love."

4) M. Scott Peck is an American psychiatrist, peace activist, and self-styled contemplative who claims that we have all the skills and techniques to build and maintain a genuine community. He speaks from his personal experience of dealing with religious communities and secular organizations. Religious communities seem hesitant to work seriously on this task: perhaps they have already achieved true community, but secular groups seem to be more willing to work on it for human and economic reasons. When people are trying to confront the issues and work at resolving them patiently, it can be, as Peck claims, a genuine "mystical" experience. It is doubtful that he is talking about contemplation in the sense which St. John of the Cross defines it as "a secret, peaceful and loving inflow of God which, if accepted, sets the heart on fire with love." (Dark Night, Bk.1, Ch.10, par. 6).

5) St. Thérèse of Lisieux, although she died over a hundred

years ago, can genuinely be considered a prophetic voice of Spirituality. She influenced the Second Vatican Council calling everyone to holiness of life. In 1997 she was named a Doctor of the Church by Pope John Paul II. She is called a "Mystic of the Ordinary" who makes intimacy with God accessible to all through her "Little Way" of surrender and gratitude. She discovered her unique vocation in the Church within her Carmelite calling.

Paying attention to her own deepest desires, which she saw as given to her by God, she wondered why He would put in her heart such "foolish" longings:

- the desire to be a priest and yet to admire the humility of St. Francis
- the longing to enlighten others as did the Prophets and Doctors
- the wish to be an Apostle and a missionary of the Gospel on all five continents
- the dream of being a martyr.

There was no hesitation in Thérèse to assign these desires to God and then struggle in prayer to make sense of them.

"Yes, I have found my place in the Church, and it is you, O my God, who has given me this place; in the heart of the Church, my Mother, I shall be love. Thus, I shall be everything, and thus my dream will be realized." (Story of a Soul; manuscript B)

St. Thérèse inspires us to explore, search out, and discover our place in the Church. She encourages us to dream dreams and to see possibilities beyond our human capacity, but attainable through the grace of God and the Spirit of Jesus.

A YOUNG AFRICAN RESPONDS

I would like to conclude these reflections on the Carmelite Charism and on the Future of the Church with a response of a young Nigerian Carmelite student, Brother Canice Mary Azuoma who attended the presentations of the Tangaza Symposium and is now a respected Carmelite priest serving in his native land of Nigeria.

Fr. Canice Azuoma,OCD

IN PRAISE OF THE MYSTIC

Talk of the authentic mystic?
Who is that one?
'Tis the one
Who has "tasted" and "seen',
Who continues to "taste" and "see"
-In day-to-day humdrum, ups, and downs of life-
The goodness, "the Loving-kindness of the heart of our God."
And who, daily empowered
By this profound "tasting" and "seeing,"
Plunges her/his self deeper into existential concerns.

Hence,
'Tis the authentic mystic

Who'll have the steel-in-the-spine
To trek from the joy-filled Emmaus road
Back to the fear-fraught Jerusalem place.

'Tis the authentic mystic
Whose Incarnation-Cross-Resurrection Spirituality
Who'll serve as a sure foundation
For novel but realistic paradigms
In a world of pluralism
'Tis the authentic mystic
Who'll tell me true stories –

> Formative, Educative, Value-full Liberating stories,
> Flowing from the mystic's own rich experiences.

'Tis the authentic mystic, who,
Rediscovering the feminine face of God,
Labors untiringly that this all-beauty face
Might shine forth in fuller splendor
On the countenances of women
(as well as men) of the third millennium.

> The whereabouts of the authentic mystic?
> Gone – really gone, are the yesteryears
> When in no other place than
> Four-walled nunneries and monasteries
> We frantically sought and adored
> The pious, withdrawn mystic.

For the authentic mystic of the third millennium,
We need strain our necks no longer!

He/she lives and moves amidst us –
(Not only in clerical and religious hoods)
But more so – matter-of-factly, in:
The scientifico-technical genius, the politician,
The business entrepreneur – small and great,
The media/computer wizard, the educator, the student,
The body-soul-spirit healer, the patient,
And even in the next-door neighbor – young or old!

Mind you, the mystic isn't a superhuman:
The mystic hasn't got ready-made answers
To all human woes and queries,
But holds – like us all – precious treasures
In earthen, fragile, wares –
Knowing too well, as flesh and blood,
The perennial tug-of-war
'Tween the fallen and redeemed self within.

Nonetheless,
'Tis the same authentic mystic
Who, with high-held-head, standing confidently
On the threshold of the third millennium,
Becomes a living, evocative symbol of possibilities:
Of pluriformity in a dividing world,
Of mutual collaboration in a chauvinistic world,
Of hope in a despairing world,
Of faith in a doubting world, ...
And healing Love for an ailing world.

Yes.
Rahner was, and is right. (God bless him!)

The Christian of the 'morrow
Cannot but be a mystic – the authentic one.
For, in the hollow of the mystic's palms,
As it were – I dare to claim –
The Future of the world – Nay the third millennium,
lies!

Canice Mary, 15/4/99

MERGING CHARISM AND CULTURE

Culture is an elusive reality – challenging to pin down and unusual in expression. The Carmelite culture of "interior prayer" speaks to us in many ways and different places; it is a challenge to open our hearts to new possibilities and be faithful to its biblical essence. We have already shared our experience of the Ugandan culture of welcome that surprisingly overflows into the liturgy. Charism and culture can often merge into one another. In Uganda, especially out in the bush, women are the ones who cultivate the small gardens that are crucial for their families. Many people were surprised to find a woman, Lillian, among our little group of missionaries, and when she met with some local women, one of them spoke out a little brashly and asked, "Does she know how to dig"? The reference was, of course, to her ability to dig in the garden. Lillian thought for a few moments and responded, "I dig in papers," indicating her work in re-organizing the Diocesan health service.

Going into a hardware store or many other shops in Kampala, I was surprised that items on sale had no price tags. Later, I was enlightened that three different prices exist, depending on who you are – a thin African, a fat African, or a muzungu. Knowing that information is essential, as it can lead to some pleasant exchanges of bartering and the possibility of having the first quote revised and of making a good bargain. The shopkeepers usually enjoy the muzungu who is willing to hassle with them.

Another more harsh reality is that of poverty in developing countries. In Uganda, the ordinary man out in the country survives on about $2.00 a day. The woman of the house needs to be an excellent gardener to provide maize, beans, and bananas for the family meals. Still, the survival reality remains a significant influence on life in general and how they think and judge.

Enriching the Church with our charisms means that the missionary must also recognize where the people are open to the ways of the spirit. Women and men working silently digging in the garden, walking long journeys on poor roads, waiting patiently for assistance in hospitals and clinics, in government offices, and at Church rectories, provide natural opportunities for silent communion with God our Father, and hope in His mysterious Providence. Jeremiah, the Old Testament prophet, faced poverty and persecution but still was able to pray in hope.

"But I will call this to mind, as my reason to have hope: the favors of the Lord are not exhausted, His mercies are not spent; they are renewed each morning, so great is his faithfulness. My portion is the Lord, says my soul; therefore, will I hope in him."

(Lamentations 3.21-24)

SONG AND PRAYER

"Don't fence me in" was the song I referred to at the beginning of this chapter. It is one of my favorites since it recalls for me the joy of openness of territory for a horseman and the much more comprehensive openness of the mysterious reality of God, the source of all life.

"Give me land, lots of land, 'neath the starry skies above,
Don't fence me in!
Let me be by myself in the evening breezes,
Listen to the murmur of the cottonwood trees,
Send me off forever, but I ask you, please!
Don't fence me in."

Praise God! I often liked to sit on a bench outside the Rectory at Kyengeza in the late evenings, enjoying the quiet breeze and hearing the murmur, not of the cottonwoods, but of the mango or eucalyptus trees. It was a naturally prayerful moment, not unlike Elijah, who, after the fierce wind, the earthquake, and the fire, perceived the presence of God in the "tiny whispering sound" (1 Kings 19.13).

7 HUMAN DEVELOPMENT

"Ekittibwa kibe ekya Patri, ...
(Glory be to the Father ...)

As we delight in the beauty of our Carmelite charism, we cannot close our eyes to the reality of the peoples' human condition. The truth of a survival culture, stark poverty, disease, polluted wells, and dirty water shouts out loud and clear. The spiritual ideals cannot hide or quench the thirst for essential human development.

Uganda is a developing country, and it has made significant advances both on the national and international levels. "COMESA" is the name given to the efforts to set up an East African common market of Uganda, Kenya, and Tanzania, as well as Sudan, Zambia, Mozambique, Ethiopia, and Eritrea. It originated in Kampala in 1993, and despite great hopes, it is struggling to deliver on its promise. It is a beginning and a commitment.

Following the turbulent years after independence and the oppressive regime of Idi Amin, there is now a stable government. Like every leadership, it has its limitations, bringing peace and growth. Many people, especially the poorer people out in the bush, have a great love and respect for the President, Yoweri Museveni, once a rebel leader but revered by many as the Liberator of Uganda.

There is surprising cooperation between Church and State. Many schools, set up by missionaries and religious, were unable to continue due to a lack of funds. They now receive support from the government. People now refer to this arrangement as 'church founded, government aided' schools. Likewise, in the AIDS crisis, the Bishops and the Government came to a compromise agreement about the use of condoms, expressed in publicly displayed posters as "Condoms for the careless; Abstinence for the wise," not a perfect solution in the eyes of the Church, but a suitable arrangement before the harsh reality of AIDS and its devastating effect on families.

Let us now look at areas of human development where our mission has tried to keep in mind both the ideals of the Church and the reality of suffering people.

HEALING OF BODY AND SPIRIT

From our initial contact with the mission at Kyengeza, we thought that setting up a medical clinic would provide for some of the urgent needs of the people. But the priests we consulted seemed to be strangely unenthusiastic about this project. We even included providing a clinic in our original budget for the mission. However, further consultation with the Diocesan leaders advised us to move slowly. It seems that there were many clinics in the diocese that were not operating efficiently. When Bishop Mukwaya took note of the character and ability of our lay volunteer, Lillian, he asked for her to assist at the Diocesan Health office with the task of re-organizing the existing health clinics in a better way. Soon afterward, she was appointed Diocesan Health Director.

Although we were not too happy that she would not be with us at Kyengeza, we knew she would do well. She continued to reside at the mission and assist the Xaverian Youth group and the growing OCDS group. She gave excellent service to the Diocese with her great love for the sick and, with her organizational skills, was instrumental in renewing many of the health services.

Sister Antonia got her Ugandan Nursing credential and continued her health services from the convent. She also worked at a newly established health center in the nearby trading center of Zigoti. Our parish leader Mark Gingo opened and ran that clinic under the patronage of St Jacinta in memory of his little daughter, Jacinta, who died early in life. Sr. Antonia also used her many talents in helping the local school children, especially from our newly constructed Little Flower Kindergarten school.

Sr. Antonia with handicapped children

Sometimes the children needed more care than the immediate attention of the nurse. Sr. Antonia set up the St. Teresa's Home for those who needed extra care. Likewise, when she visited the family homes of our SACC (sponsored) children, she discovered other handicapped children, who were sometimes left uncared for and could benefit from a more prolonged treatment than they would get at home. In many poor places, parents do not always know how handicapped children can be helped and sometimes are ashamed to seek assistance. Sr. Antonia's ministry to these was a real blessing; the parents trusted Sister and knew their children were in good hands.

Bridget with her family and Sister Antonia.

Near our parish of St. Kizito, there was a family with a little girl, Bridget by name, who could not stand upright or walk but always wanted to play with her sisters and brothers. Our lay volunteer, Tim McCormack, who often passed by their house on foot, enjoyed meeting the children and knew little Bridget's condition. Tim himself constructed a simple therapy contraption for her and became a hero to her, her little brother, "Dulu," and all her family.

Then Sr. Antonia provided Bridget with a wheelchair and enrolled her in the Little Flower School.

The other school children loved to help her and guide the wheelchair over the rugged pathways to the school. They also made sure that she would join in all the school activities. Many were blessed by helping little Bridget; she became a catalyst for changing how many looked upon a handicapped person.

Healing takes place in many ways. We must not forget the Sacraments of healing, the Sunday Masses, the Anointing of the sick, the sacrament of Penance by which the Lord removes the burden of sin and refreshes the heart by His mercy. One incident stands out in my memories. A family messenger came pleading with me to visit a dying man out in the bush. I got as far as I could in our green truck and then proceeded on foot. Soon I was followed by a group of children, curious to know what the muzungu priest, moving along sprightly, was doing. Following the directions, I reached the small, poor home of the sick man. His bed was a mattress on the main room floor, and the wife and neighbors were praying together for him. The only light came from the open door and a small window.

After a brief greeting, I started the prayers for the sick from my ritual. By this time, the children were at the door and window, looking in to see what the muzungu was doing. They were blocking the light from coming into the already dark room. No one, except me, took any notice of them, and I went to the door to try to hush them away so that I could see the prayers in my book. They ran off laughing, and of course, when I went back into the room, the children returned. It was a lost cause trying to read the prayers, so I began with the Our Father and Hail Mary; then, the Lord inspired me to sing the well-known Ekittibwa (The 'Glory be' in Luganda). Everyone knew the simple melody and joined in; even the poor man who was dying pushed himself up to a sitting position to do his part in the hymn. It was the happiest last rites I ever administered in my many years as a priest. The singing brought great joy to the family and the dying man. Here are the words in Luganda with an English translation we sang in Kenya.

Ekitiibwa kibe ekya Patri, n'ekya Mwana, n'ekya Mwoyo Mutukirivu, Nga bwe kyaliwo olubereberye, Na kaakono, na bulijjo, emirembe n'emirembe. Amina.

Give praise to the Father Almighty, to His Son Jesus Christ the Lord, To the Spirit who dwells in our hearts, both now and forever, Amen.

Singing and praising God is a beautiful way to meet the Lord. Recognition of the Three Divine Persons is at the heart of our faith, the faith which we received at Baptism and which will become our eternal joy in heaven.

EDUCATION

If you want to feed a child for a day, give him a mango.
If you want to provide for her for a month, plant maize.
If you want to help him for a lifetime, educate him.

I have seen posters with similar messages in many Development offices in Uganda. It gives us the news of a value appreciated in Uganda and worldwide. Education is crucial for human growth. In Uganda, children are everywhere and, consequently, we have lots of schools: kindergarten, primary, secondary, and a few good higher educational facilities. Some are privately owned and operated; others are public or have that distinctive Ugandan arrangement "Church founded; government-aided." Most students need "school fees," and all need extra help even when they are government-run or government-aided. "School fees" we soon realized is another urgent need among our people.

Tim McCormack with two small children

Children love mangos and sugar cane; many, on their way to school, find a good mango tree that will provide some nourishment, especially when there is no food at home for breakfast. Maize and beans and plantains (cooking bananas} are considered staple foods for any meal, but education is for the whole of life and is recognized by all as a true blessing for their families. In meeting the constant appeal from parents and the children themselves for school fees, we were helped by many generous benefactors in America and by some in Ireland, who sponsored one, or two or occasionally three children for their education. This program got the name SACC (Sponsor a child, Carmelite). Its inspiration was the CFCA program that Fr Lawrence OFM Cap. was leading in the adjacent parish of Busungu. We developed our style with great help from Sr.

Antonia and the many overseas benefactors; it became a tremendous blessing for many of the children of our mission.

The sponsor donated a monthly amount to support the child's education, $15.00, $20.00, or $25.00. That money goes to pay the school fees, and if there is something over and above, we put it into a fund for Birthday group celebrations, Christmas parties with gifts, and Retreat Days for the children.

On their part, the children write three letters each year to the sponsor to let them know about their progress at school, about themselves and their families. The children often need to be pushed and coached on writing the letters, but we always saw it as a good teaching opportunity and cultivating a good relationship with the sponsor. It was a two-way street between little ones and the sponsors, who often found joy in communicating with their African friends. This letter connection was made through our Mission Office at the Carmelite Monastery in Oakville, Napa Valley, and our excellent staff at Kyengeza.

We were fortunate to hire a trained social worker to assist Sr. Antonia on this task and many other aspects of the sponsorship program: Sharon Najjengo. Sharon had come to us seeking help to complete her Social Studies at the University.

I found a generous sponsor in California, and then I made a deal with Sharon. When she completed her course at the University, she would come to work for us for a year, and we would have the first choice to hire her if we wished. Both sides were happy with this arrangement, and Sharon became a capable and reliable assistant to Sr. Antonia. Another great helper at the mission was Annett Muyira, one of the teachers at St. Kizito's Primary school. In California, at the Mission office, we also had dedicated secretaries, Helga Nice and Bill Zdanoski, who loved this missionary work, and many local volunteers helped.

The Uganda Educational system works in conjunction with the Catholic school efforts according to that pithy phrase "Church founded; Government aided." Education is taken seriously by the Church, as is evident from the fact that the associate priest in the parish is the one named as "Priest in charge of Schools." This title gives him a specific and challenging ministry with his other priestly duties. The Church retains ownership of the schools; the government provides an impressive syllabus and pays the teachers. The parents have to contribute in many ways to the upkeep and running of the schools. Most parents recognize the value of a good education, but many are also too poor to help. Especially in rural areas, parents would often keep their children at home to help during the planting and harvesting times. Keeping food on the table is often an urgent need that easily takes precedence to the long-term goal of a good education.

In the beginning, as we provided school fees directly to the parents, we discovered that not all of it went to education. More immediate family needs often claimed the available school fees. Consequently, we gave the school fees directly to the school and not to the parents of the children. We made mistakes, but we also learned quickly. The program developed well under the leadership of Sr. Antonia. The children were required to "pay back" by helping at the parish or with the catechists at the out-stations. We always tried to have practical gifts for the children at Christmas or birthday celebrations. They loved to receive gifts of clothes and shoes, but the families were thrilled when they brought home a new hoe, a shovel, or a mattress. It was a joyful experience for us too – to see how they rolled up their mattresses, tied them securely with banana fibers, and carried them home proudly.

A happy boy carrying a mattress home.

The Carmelite Sisters also had sponsors from Austria, and, at one stage, we had more than 200 children in the program. Sr. Antonia also organized Retreat days for the children in which they willingly participated. A further development was the School Lunch program. That developed unplanned when we discovered that many children came to school without breakfast. The sponsored children's school fees assured them of a simple lunch, but the other children were often without breakfast and lunch. They envied the "Carmelite" children, and inevitably bad feelings came forth. To avoid this situation and provide a simple lunch for all the children in the school, we began the School Lunch program. Again, our overseas supporters responded with incredible generosity. We extended the program to all the schools of the mission, and it was a blessing to be able to help so many children.

Later, we decided that a kindergarten school could greatly help the children entering the school system. Sr. Antonia once again was a significant force in its planning and development. It is called the Little Flower School, and although its original goal was to provide ready students for entrance to our own St. Kizito Primary school, not all parents sent their children to St Kizito's.

Other parents were so happy with our efforts that they requested we add a boarding section for their little ones! We did not go along with that idea. But soon, Sr. Antonia was planning a particular home for sick children and others she had discovered on her parish visitations who needed much more care than they were receiving at home. It was called St. Teresa's Home and was a typical example of Sr. Antonia's energy, love, and creativity for the poor and sick children of the mission. As well as St. Kizito's Primary school, we also had St. Ambrose's Secondary School in the parish compound, where many of our sponsored children attended. We tried to help all the schools in the mission parish by providing water tanks, latrines, maintenance of buildings, and the SACC program.

"WINE TO WATER" — "WATER HOPE"

Clean water is another great need of the mission. From the first days of our time in Uganda, we could not but notice the many children who carried yellow "jerry cans" of water, some balanced precariously on their heads.

After school hours, it was a regular chore to go to the watering hole and bring home some of that precious liquid. Even the little ones joined their older brothers and sisters, with their own much smaller containers, to do their part for the family's needs. Unfortunately, not all the sources of water were in good condition. Many were unprotected and also used by animals. The result from using this contaminated water was disease and poor health, and the children themselves were the most susceptible to these. In this context, we might mention that the life expectancy of the people of Uganda at that time was 48 years! Many factors contributed to this sad situation, but contaminated water and AIDS were the main culprits.

A little girl carrying jerry cans of water.

How could we help? Our first substantial effort was to provide "boreholes" – as they call them in Uganda: that is, to dig deep wells for clean water. This provision was an expensive project as each one would cost at least $10,000.00, but it was an urgent need. Another appeal to our USA benefactors and, providentially, we met with Steve Tomkovich.

Steve gives a big check to Fr. Reginald for Water Hope Ministry.
Steve's wife, Tracy, and daughter, Alison are also in the picture

Steve was a Religious Education volunteer teacher at St. Apollinaris Parish in Napa, California. Len Powers spent some time as a volunteer in Nairobi with me and together we visited Uganda before the mission began. Len was a guest speaker at Steve's Religious Education class and spoke about his experience in Africa and the need for clean water.

The teacher and the pupils were duly impressed and wanted to help. Steve reflected on the situation with his wife Tracy, and they decided to start up a particular Foundation for the needs of clean water in missionary countries.

Many of Steve's business clients were in the Napa Valley of California, as was the Carmelite Mission office at Oakville. Steve decided to enlist the assistance of his winemaker business friends and partners and came up with the fortuitous name for the foundation – "Wine to Water." This venture was an inspired and effective decision for Steve's own business and the needs of his missionary friends in many lands. Their goodness reached Uganda, India, and Nepal.

Later, Steve and his daughter Alison and another business associate, Wayne Conner, visited our Mission in Uganda and experienced life among the people they supported so generously. As the work of his Foundation broadened and many others outside the Wine Country became involved, they changed the foundation's name to "Water Hope." Many times, when I was wearing my "Wine to Water" cap or shirt, I was accosted by someone saying, "You have that sign on backward; should it not read "Water to Wine"? I was happy to explain its origin and promote our cause.

With such great help, we started digging our first borehole at Kyengeza itself. The presence of big machinery drilling deep into the earth was a great fascination for all, especially for the children of the nearby St. Kizito's Primary school. But even more excitement followed when the clean water gushed out for the first time. The children cautiously tasted it, then happily washed their faces in the lovely fresh, clean water; they jumped up and down, blessed themselves with it, and praised God for so great a gift! - Holy water indeed!

We agreed with the local sub parish leaders that they would care for the protection and maintenance of the borehole and would charge a nominal fee to the users. They readily agreed to these terms, but the follow-through was poor. Consequently, they came to the bwanamukulu (the pastor) with their sad story when some breakdown occurred. What could he do? Remind them of their part of the bargain, urge them to take greater responsibility for its maintenance, and then help them with the repair costs. Interestingly, when the muzungu priests were no longer at the mission, the local people did step up with new energy and responsibility, thanks be to God.

We dug a few more boreholes – at Magonga, Mpirrigwa, and Bukalagi – and repaired an old one at Kysengese. The Sisters also funded one at the nearby trading center of Kikonge (see our book cover photo). The many requests for help for clean water made us look at other options to the expensive, difficult to arrange, and slow borehole solution. What we came up with was the large plastic tank! We could harvest the rainwater; the heavy downpours during the rainy seasons would fill up the tanks quickly. Besides, they were much less expensive than boreholes. We could purchase them easily in Kampala, have them delivered to the mission at Kyengeza, and then deliver them in our own Nissan truck to the needy parishioners. It was a joyful task. We focused on older people who would have a hard time going to the well or a good source and then getting the heavy jerry can back home. It was also a precious gift to our catechists in the out-lying sub-parishes, and they appreciated them very much.

Fr. David driving the pickup with a tank well-tied in the back

To receive a tank, the recipient needed a good solid concrete base and a galvanized roof on their house from where the water would flow to the collecting shoot and reach the tank. The parishioners were happy to provide these requirements, which were relatively inexpensive and straightforward. We encouraged them to share the precious liquid with the older or poorer neighbors, who did not have a galvanized roof on their homes. We also tried to provide tanks for all the schools in the parish and the sub-parishes. The only problem was that the tank filters were not as effective as we had hoped, and some of the dirt from the roofs would gradually seep into the tanks. A simple solution to that problem was to clean out the tanks thoroughly at the beginning of the two rainy seasons of each year. That was a good solution, but many tank recipients balked at using all that good rainfall and were willing to put up with a bit of mud in the tank.

Searching for other possibilities for clean water, we discovered the "Water with Blessings" program. Its spirituality relates to the story of the Samaritan woman (John, Chapter 4) – much loved by St. Teresa of Avila, and it promotes the use of small, lightweight 'Sawyer One' filters. It targets the parents of children under five years of age who are at high risk from unclean water. They are not costly, approximately $60.00 each. The home base of this great program is in Middletown, Kentucky, and the director is Sister Larraine Lauter. They are doing an excellent service to people in any developing country needing clean water.

On our Missionary Pilgrimage of 2014, we brought 50 filters and organized a training session for parents at our Catechist Hall in Kyengeza. The parents attending were mainly mothers, but a few men, including a Muslim father, also participated. One of our pilgrims, Sarah Kate from Yountville, California, was born in Uganda and returned to her native land for the first time in 20 years. She spoke Luganda and was an ideal member of our Training team with Sr. Antonia, Sharon Najjengo, and local teacher Annet Muyira. Other pilgrims who played a significant role in the training were Dianne Hamm OCDS from New Mexico, and Kiyoshi Sakakura from California.

Our pilgrims enjoyed this direct missionary "outreach" very much; the parents were delighted with their gifts and responded enthusiastically to the project. It did not just consist of handing out the filters, training, and maintenance; it also had the formation of "Water Women"- little groups of mothers who would help and encourage one another in benefiting from this project.

The obvious connection to the Samaritan woman story and the promise of Jesus to give her "Living Water" was easy to make. Likewise, the "four waters" of St. Teresa of Avila, describing the growth of prayer, was another inspiring connection to our water ministry. The search goes on - for clean water and the "Water of

Life." Benefactors and mission supporters readily understand this great need and continue to respond generously.

CONSTRUCTION

Before finishing this chapter, we must recall the various construction efforts that lifted the people's spirit and developed a greater community awareness. We provided simple homes for many old and poor people whose homes were in poor condition or collapsed in a storm. Constructions built with mud bricks last about ten years; schools needed concrete floors or new outdoor latrines, and sub-parishes were always hoping for a suitable building for the Sacred Liturgy. All of these grabbed our attention, and it was a joy to help with simple constructions ideal for a developing country.

One of the poorest sub-parishes was undoubtedly Magonga. There was no Church building. We met in the school for Mass. Behind the table that served as the altar was a blackboard with a Cross chalked on it. Wandering around the compound, I noticed what appeared to be an abandoned foundation for some building project that never materialized. I inquired about it, and they told me it was the foundation of the Church, but because of lack of funds, they abandoned the project. At the end of Mass that day, I promised to help them find funds for a new Church. Overjoyed by my promise and feeling like a politician who promises lots, it tempted me to add other possible areas where I might find help for them; however, thanks to God, I refrained! On the way home with my trusty homily translator, Andrew Bimpebwa, as we swung around a corner going into one of the villages of the sub-parish, there in the middle of the dirt road stood a disheveled looking man, standing beside a jerry can, waving me down. My first thought was that he had imbibed too much local brew and needed a lift. I stopped, and he picked up the jerry can and approached the truck to speak with me. It was only then I recognized him!

It was Lawrence, the local Sabbakristu (the head Christian), who attended my Mass and had made some gracious remarks at the end. He greeted me again and then presented me with the jerry can, with the top of it cut off and three quarters filled with water; "Look," as he pointed into the can, "this is for you"! I could hardly believe my eyes; a live, nice-sized fish was in the jerry can! I got out of the truck, took the jerry can, and gave it to Andrew to keep it safe for the journey home over the rough, bush-country road. As we moved off, Lawrence called out, "bring me back my jerry can"! We got home safely and presented our catch of the day to our cooks, Judith and Felicity. They too were delighted, and Judith announced, "we will have it for supper tonight." It was a great meal.

We did get some good benefactors to help; a small sub-parish Church is not expensive, maybe less than $10,000.00, and the local people were always willing to help by providing water, stones, and sand if these were locally available. Then on the day of blessing the new Church, since everyone wanted to attend, we had to set up a temporary outside tent for the Mass and the big crowd, and from there, move to the blessing of the Church.

We were fortunate to have our Provincial, Fr. Gerald Werner, visiting at that time; he came along to participate and helped at the Baptism of twenty-four new little Christians. Even though it was a busy time for him because of pending local elections, the local parliamentarian also came. He brought a case of beer and a supply of soda – good electioneering! It was a joyous occasion for everyone, and we all went home tired and happy after a grand celebration.

Magonga was also the recipient of a water tank for the school and later for the parish, a borehole. We helped the school in many ways, including building an outdoor privy and getting sponsors for many local orphaned children. A large number of orphans in the area resulted from the AIDS scourge. A surprising fallout from helping Magonga so much was the particular envy expressed by one of the catechists to me: "You love Magonga too much"! I took note and ensured I would help every sub-parish so far as funds were available.

Another remote sub-parish was Kito, also trying to build their little Church. Fr. Colm came home one Sunday from celebrating Mass there and announced he would never go there again. Apparently, during the announcements before the final blessing of the Mass, someone questioned the use of funds collected, and it turned into a very nasty and heated debate that Fr. Colm felt was entirely out of place at a Sunday Mass. There were some antipathies between two factions of the sub-parish. However, they seemed to have resolved it as the construction continued and half the roof was in place. But one stormy night, it came down, and much of the blaming and anger resurfaced. We took an extended time-out from that building project until we found a better solution by getting a different construction group to finish the job. Then a few days before the celebration and blessing, I was informed that the local Chairman would be the honored guest and would like to speak at the function. The local Chairman happened to be a Muslim woman.

That gave me some worries, not because she was a woman, but that was the time when Pope Benedict had made some remarks about Muhammad that were considered offensive to the Muslim community throughout the world. I worried if that controversy had reached Kito and if it would cast a damper on our celebrations. I tried to relax and put it in the hands of the Lord. We had a great gathering and lovely celebrations in the typical Ugandan style. To cap it all, our Local Chairperson was most gracious; she congratulated the sub-parish people for their construction, stating how important it was to have their own place of worship and wished them every blessing for the future. What a relief! We all went home happy and grateful to God for all His goodness.

8

VOCATIONS and the FUTURE

"Hello, darkness, my old friend..."

We were not in any hurry to start formation work, even if it did cross our minds from time to time. Bishop Mukwaya advised us not to consider accepting possible vocations to our Carmelite community for at least three or four years. There was wisdom in his observation. Then, almost exactly after three years, some young men began to manifest an interest in joining our community. Most of them were from our sub-parish of Kyengeza and one young man from the sub-parish of Magonga. It was interesting and exciting that they felt attracted to our way of life. We dialogued with them and tried to discern together if it were a real call to the Carmelite priesthood or brotherhood. The very first one on whom we put great hopes was Andrew Bimpebwa, whom we have mentioned already as a willing helper at our out-station Masses and always a joy to have around Kyengeza. He went through an extended trial period of postulancy, attending classes at Jinja and, while there, staying with the Comboni community. Later in Nairobi, when he

115

lived in our Carmelite community, he attended courses at Tangaza College. After doing his novitiate in Malawi, Brother Andrew of the Sacred Heart of Jesus made his profession as a Carmelite brother on the feast of our Lady of Mount Carmel in 2009.

Fr. Godfrey Chandya Lega

Fr. Godfrey Chandya Lega was a surprise applicant because he was already an ordained priest of the diocese of Arua. He did his postulancy with us at Kyengeza and then requested permission to go to Nigeria for his novitiate. Some of our young men in Kenya had gone to Nigeria for their early training as novices and found it very demanding in many ways. Fr. Godfrey felt he needed a challenging novitiate experience since he came to us already formed in the Diocesan seminary. He did very well there and returned to Kyengeza for his profession of vows at Kyengeza on August 22, 2008. Even if Bro. Andrew was the first postulant from the Mission, Fr. Godfrey is undoubtedly the first Ugandan to make his profession in Uganda. We do not forget two other Ugandans who joined the order in Kenya before the mission in Uganda began at Kyengeza, namely, Fr. Joseph Baru and Fr. Richard Opendi.

We were now considering the building of a small house for our postulants in one of the sub parishes. Initially, our imagination focused on Ttumbu as a possible site; it was on a hill, clearly visible from our veranda at Kyengeza where we often prayed the Divine Office. We considered it ideal for the initial Carmelite experience for our new applicants. Talking with Bishop Zziwa about this possibility, he welcomed it and then suggested that we should consider the sub-parish of Kabule, which was much bigger than Ttumbu and more central to the parish. He asked us to draw up a draft proposal of what we wished and that he would consider it. That was easy to do and we duly presented it at his office in Mityana.

At the same time, Sr. Antonia hoped to build an appropriately sized home for sick or handicapped children she encountered on her parish visitations, also for the children of our Little Flower School who needed extra care. She, too, presented a proposal for the Bishop's scrutiny and approval. We waited patiently for a word from the Bishop, but nothing came. Had he forgotten about the Carmelites? Then, Sr. Antonia asked me if I would mind checking in with the Bishop.

Not keen on approaching Bishop Zziwa, as we priests, knew how busy he was and how deliberately he proceeded on Diocesan matters, I declined her invitation. But that did not deter Sr. Antonia; she decided to call him herself and encountered some episcopal wrath for her "haughty" impatience! My reaction was a sincere "Thanks be to God I did not call him"! We waited and waited and wondered how long more.

On our part, we had to have something set up for the coming academic year as we now had five young men eager to begin their postulancy stage of formation. Postulancy proceeds in various ways; sometimes, it is done separately from other studies, focusing on ministry; or the authorities may wish to combine it with activities on the college or philosophy level. We now concentrated on Jinja, where we were fortunate to rent a building from the Claretian community, from where our young men could attend the P.C.J. (the Philosophical College of Jinja) and at the same time live in a Carmelite community setting. That would tide us over until we could build our separate residence. Fr. Edmond Shabani was willing to accompany and direct the postulants at the rented house. That meant that there would be two muzungu priests, Fr. Paul and myself, and the diocesan priest, Fr. Charles Matumbwe, to serve the parish at Kyengeza. We forgot about the postulant residence at Ttumbu or Kabule! The use of the newly rented house gave us time to observe the P.C.J. set-up and explore possibilities for a more permanent home.

P.C.J. is a consortium of religious communities who have come together for the early formation of their young men at the level of college or philosophy. It also serves as an extended postulancy stage for many of our students before their canonical novitiate. That is slightly different from the traditional method of having a short postulancy experience in a separate house before moving on to college stage studies or the novitiate residence. Tangaza College in Nairobi is a similar consortium-style college for Theology and other courses for men or women religious, just a few minutes walk from our International community on Langata Road. Our International Carmelite College in Rome is another option for theological studies, and some of our Ugandan students have studied there.

We were somewhat familiar with P.C.J. because our first postulant, Andrew Bimpebwa, studied there as he lived at the Comboni community within the P.C.J. compound while discerning his Carmelite vocation. Andrew continued his formation and studies in Nairobi at the Tangaza Institute of Spirituality and is now a solemnly professed member of our community of Duruelo in Jinja.

As well as the Comboni community, a few other religious congregations have their residence within the P.C.J. compound and built their own formation house there. At this stage, two lots were available for purchase on which a community could develop their residence. Other religious communities had purchased land outside the P.C.J. compound. A further exciting option was the willingness of Bishop Willigers to lease us one of the two lots belonging to the diocese and adjacent to the P.C.J. We explored all possibilities; the purchase of the plot within the compound was expensive and not favored by our Provincial Council. We also discovered how difficult it was to purchase land nearby.

Finally, with a certain amount of frustration but with a lot of hope, we returned to Bishop Willigers to see if his original offer still held. The Bishop was always gracious and willingly provided us with the small lot of two to three acres, looking out on Lake Victoria and adjacent to the P.C.J. fence. All we had to do was pay off the settlers who had parked themselves there. We did this without problems and moved to the next step.

For the building of our new residence, Sr. Antonia showed another talent in helping draw up a draft outline for the builder, Robert Irumba, with whom the Sisters and we were familiar from various constructions at Kyengeza. We deliberately planned a modest building, expecting an intake of five postulants each year that, with a likely fall-out of two or three, would leave us with six students in three years, plus the new group entering. At this early stage, we did not foresee finally professed students or ordained priests returning to reside at the Jinja house. Kyengeza was still in our hands and would be ideal for students getting pastoral experience during their summer vacation and for the assignment of those who had completed formation.

"Duruelo" – House of Formation
Spain 1568 (left) to Uganda 2008 (right)
The cradle of the Discalced Carmelite Friars, inspiration of our Formation
house in Jinja, continues to remind us of the simple creative fidelity of our
founders.

The building of the new house proceeded without any significant problems. We chose to call it "Duruelo" in memory of the first house of the Reformed Friars in Spain, where St. John of the Cross ministered so happily and what pleased St. Teresa so greatly. The location is stunning, in sight of Lake Victoria and the source of the Nile, and convenient to P.C.J. – a short walk for our students. Qualified Carmelite Friars had the opportunity of teaching at P.C.J. as Fr. Stephen did during his time at Duruelo. Everything seemed to be progressing well.

We were happy about the three possible Formation Centers for our students - P.C.J. at Jinja, Tangaza in Nairobi, and the International College in Rome. However, we still had to find a good place for the initial crucial stage of Formation, the Novitiate. We considered that Malawi (south of Tanzania) would be the best place for the Novitiate experience. It was a Mission of the Navarre Province and had many local vocations well prepared for this critical stage of training. The other option for the novices is Nigeria, but that is on the western side of the African continent and a long way from Uganda. (See a map of Africa on page 202, also a map of East African Nations on page 205).

Some Kenyan students and later some of our novices went

there when the Malawian region had no Novitiate class for that year. Here it is good to note that the natural development of religious communities is to join forces and form an East African region. Will that happen among the Carmelites of Kenya, Tanzania, Malawi, and Uganda? We must wait and see if that structure will come to fruition among our East African Carmelites.

SICKNESS STRIKES

In the fall of 2008, I became ill with what seemed to be a regular bout of malaria. It is not unusual for foreigners in Africa to come down with this disease. I was fortunate that it never bothered me in Kenya, but in the early days in Uganda, at Kasambya, I experienced it for the first time. That was when our original three missionaries, Bro. Bernard, Lillian, and I were staying at the White Fathers' parish, learning the language and getting familiar with the pastoral procedures of the diocese. When malaria strikes, you know it; you feel it in your joints and muscles; it hits you in the head and the stomach, and you must seek help as soon as possible. I was not sure what was the matter with me. But Fr. Peter, the Dutch pastor of Kasambya, knew and immediately brought me to the local clinic in the village. The blood test left no doubt, and they gave me the appropriate medication. Soon I was on the way to healing. However, after six years and several bouts of malaria, I thought I would get over this latest bout without too much difficulty. This time, however, the medication was not having any effect. I realized it was something more complicated, so I asked Fr. Larry to give me the anointing of the sick and bring me to the Diocesan clinic of St. Luke in Mityana.

After checking in at the clinic, they put me in one of the few hospital rooms attached to the clinic. I was in and out of consciousness and in and out of the bathroom. In a moment of alertness, I heard two of the Sisters discussing my condition "we cannot do anything for this man; we better send him to Nsambya" (the hospital in Kampala). I was losing a lot of blood and was very weak. St. Luke's clinic is part of the Diocesan complex, including the Cathedral, the Diocesan offices, a Priests' residence, and the Catechetical Center. My next awareness was of the local priests coming to say "Goodbye" to me, wish me well, and assure me that I will have the 'good' ambulance of Dr. Zziwa. This doctor is not the Bishop, and his 'Good' ambulance was a higher standard vehicle than the one, the old clunker that Lillian used for her ministry from the Diocesan Health office!

At that time, the road to Kampala was rough and full of potholes, and in my sick condition, I was not aware of them, traveling in the 'ambulance of Dr. Zziwa'! I was still "in and out" of consciousness, but I remember clearly the surprising song lyrics that were going through my head: *Hello, darkness, my old friend...*

Even though I always liked Simon and Garfunkel's music and songs, I was taken by surprise by the "Sounds of Silence" at this juncture of my life. What was it saying to me? Why has it come so clearly at this time? Was it connected with the writings of our beloved Carmelite Mystical Doctor of the Church, St. John of the Cross, known as the Nightingale of Fontiveros (El Ruiseñor de Fontiveros)? Many are familiar with John's "Dark Night of the Soul," but my favorite would be his "Spiritual Canticle' and of that poem, stanzas 14 and 15 in which the soul sings the praises of God, the creator.

My beloved, the mountains, and the lonely, wooded valleys,
Strange islands and resounding rivers,
The whistling of love-stirring breezes,
The tranquil night at the time of the rising dawn,

Silent music, sounding solitude,
The supper that refreshes and deepens love.

In my semi-conscious condition, I was not aware of any pot-hole discomfort; the words of the Simon-Garfunkel were comforting and surprising, but I have no idea how long I spent considering them. At the hospital, I remember only getting a variety of intravenous medications, which stopped the bleeding and gave me some relief. The next day, Sr. Antonia arrived with two Rectory staff members, Prossy and Judith, who were assigned to stay and help the patient, as is required in the Ugandan hospital tradition. Some diocesan priests also came later in the day, but I was not in any condition to visit with them. Their blessings and assurances of prayers were consoling.

Maybe their presence also prompted a strange dream. In it, one of the Diocesan priests was talking with me about my funeral arrangements. He told me, "You will be buried in the Diocesan cemetery at Mityana, in the clergy section." My response was strong and definite "No! I want you to bury me in our little plot at Kyengeza," the unmarked place where the poor people who have no property and no family receive their final resting place. I recalled those occasions' sadness, specifically of a little boy who wandered off from the group to find some wildflowers for his younger brother in the grave. The priest, in my dream, objected to my wish, claiming that "the Bishop will insist on your burial in the Priests' plot in Mityana." My reply was equally definite: "Tell the Bishop to please respect my dying wish"!

I gradually recovered and did not get my dying wish! Later, that dying wish became the desire to be interred in our community cemetery in San Jose, California. Many years earlier, as local Superior of that community, I had begun plans to set it up. Further change came when I was assigned to Arizona in 2018 and visited the Catholic cemetery of Holy Hope, where there is a particular plot for Carmelites. Maybe that will be my final resting place in this world, but as St. Monica told her son Augustine and his brother: "Bury me wherever you wish, be sure to remember me at the altar of the Mass"!

Eventually, when I returned to Kyengeza, although unaware of it myself, people noticed that I had lost my balance, and some even asked me if I had been drinking early in the morning! No, it wasn't the local brew nor any other libation; it was just some unusual effect of the illness and the medication. Fortunately, I was not dizzy and had no pain. It lasted about four months, and when I returned to California, with the help of regular therapy, I gradually got back to normal functioning without the use of a cane!

Many of our muzungu friars have been hit by one form or another of sickness. Malaria is the usual suspect, but there are other complications at work, like the side effects of the medication we take to prevent malaria. The return to the homeland is always a "desirable and effective" cure! One of the native Ugandans offered me his explanation: "You muzungus are like the exotic cattle (the better breed imported from Europe); our local cattle do not give as much milk as the exotics; they do not have as much beef on their bones but they last longer, they survive." I often wondered about those local scrawny animals who eked out a living among weeds and grass on the side of the road and, despite their poor looks, managed to survive and provide something for their owners. Indeed part of the "survival" culture of many poor countries! In my own amateur opinion, I often attributed my recovery to the "good food and good wine" of the Napa Valley.

That hardly explains the incredible energy I discovered later in my work as Mission Zelator. I took on assignments to promote the

Mission, celebrating and preaching at three to five Masses (sometimes even more). That meant I did quite a lot of traveling to the various dioceses of California and Nevada.

Back in Uganda, we decided that my return to California would be necessary for a good recovery. That was in 2008. That also meant a rigorous revision of assignments in Uganda. Luckily for us, Fr. Larry had good experience in the formation program from his time in Nairobi. So he willingly stepped up to take the duty of Superior of our formation house in Jinja with Fr. Godfrey to assist him. Fr. Edmond was recalled from Jinja and took over as acting Pastor at Kyengeza with Fr. Paul and the Diocesan priest, Fr. Charles Matumbwe, as his assistants. My Provincial, Fr Matthew Williams, advised me to take at least a three-month break in California, then extended it to six months, and after that, "we'll see"!

The new arrangement in Uganda worked out well at the beginning. The Bishop was happy with the new acting Pastor, Fr Edmond, who was fluent in Luganda and competent in organizing the parish. At this time, September 27th to be exact, Fr. Stephen Watson, who had completed his term as General Definitor in Rome, came to Jinja as promised and took over as Superior of the house and the mission. Fr. Stephen was the founding Provincial Superior of our mission and visited Kyengeza every year as Provincial and again as Definitor General. He always expressed his love for the missionary venture and his desire to serve the mission in Uganda. He remained faithful to that promise. Fr Stephen worked faithfully at Duruelo for almost two years until he fell victim to that dangerous malaria medication, Lariam. With his presence, Fr. Godfrey was freed to continue his studies in Nairobi. Fr. Edmond Shabani was officially appointed Pastor of St. Kizito's parish of Kyengeza. by the Bishop.

In California, I took over as director of the Mission Office in the Carmelite House of Prayer, Oakville, in the beautiful Napa Valley. I succeeded Fr. Reginald McSweeney, who had served so generously in that task for the previous six years. I organized a Missionary Pilgrimage to Uganda and received a warm welcome back from the people and the friars. This happy but relatively short stay gave me a sense of the natural changes under new leadership.

Yet, all was not well! Problems at the mission parish and the house of formation caused much upheaval, which necessitated the General Definitor from Rome, Fr. George Tambala, to come for a formal visitation. He acted decisively in sending Fr. Edmond back to the Congo, as he (Fr. Edmond) stated cryptically in an email to me "for farther (sic) studies,"; and the formation situation was "suspended for a year in the name of re-founding" at Duruelo. The "re-founding" year was to concentrate on Carmelite studies. At Kyengeza, Fr. Paul became "acting Pastor," but since his knowledge of the local language was limited, the Bishop moved in and took the parish back to Diocesan administration. That happened very suddenly by executive decisions that left

Fr. Matthew Williams

the priests and the people disturbed and upset. Many shed tears at this challenging time, but there was a vague hope and perhaps a verbal promise on behalf of the Bishop that in some future time, the Carmelites might return to the mission parish of St. Kizito at Kyengeza. The Provincial at that time was Fr. Matthew Williams, who seemed to be happy with the outcome for Kyengeza and Duruelo. He wrote the following explanation for publication in our Mission Newsletter of December 2012.

Dear Friends and Benefactors of our Mission,

It is with sadness that I announce that we, the Discalced Carmelite Friars, have left the parish of St. Kizito, Kyengeza, Uganda. I am sure you have several questions about this decision and the future of the Mission but let me assure you it was done with due consultation and with concern for the future of the Mission in Uganda.

We have sent three new men to the Mission to concentrate on forming our Ugandan students. And we have the word of the Bishop that at a future date when we have sufficient personnel, we will, with the Diocese, reexamine the possibility of returning to St. Kizito Parish.

Regarding donations, we first want to thank you for your prayers and great support of our Mission over the last ten years. During this time of strengthening our presence, we rely on your prayers and financial help more than ever. We are still in discussion with the Bishop as to the best way to continue our projects in helping the children and the poor of the parish. I also want to assure you that the money you so generously give will be used for that purpose.

I end by thanking you for your prayers and generosity to our Mission and assuring you of our prayers as together we continue to establish our Discalced Carmelite Order in Uganda.

Your brother in Christ,
Father Matthew Williams OCD, Provincial

Not everything went as smoothly as it appears. As well as the emotional tears and sadness already mentioned, there was also deep disappointment. On our part, we thought that there was an excellent opportunity for a native Carmelite priest to take over as Pastor of Kyengeza – Fr. Richard Opendi.

Richard, a native of Tororo in Uganda, had entered the Carmelites in Nairobi, Kenya, before the mission in Uganda began. Like his fellow Ugandan Carmelite in Kenya, Fr. Joseph Baru, Fr Richard longed to minister among his own people. As his Vocation Director in Kenya, I knew him well and recommended him for the position of Pastor. However, Bishop Zziwa claimed that Richard was dismissed from the Major Seminary in Uganda, and on that basis, he could not, nor would not, accept him as Pastor. It is, of course, the prerogative of the local Bishop to accept or reject the person proposed by the religious Superior. But Richard stated clearly, that he had never been in the Major Seminary, nor had he ever been dismissed. The Bishop remained adamant in his own opinion. Richard had attended the Minor Seminary in Mubende, and the Bishop seems to have confused him with another Richard - Fr. Richard Lubaale - a Camillian. Fr Lubaale died in recent years as a comparatively young priest.

Unfortunately, our men negotiating with the Bishop did not know Fr. Opendi, did not consult with those who did and accepted the Bishop's version. Fr. Richard also strongly asserted his side of the story; both cannot be correct. Justice requires a thorough investigation, and resolution of this difference is needed. The "re-founding" plan sounds somewhat hollow in the context of this conflict and has left unhealed wounds despite the best efforts to accept God's will.

This story reminds me of the conflict between Cardinal McIntyre and Fr. Edward Leahy in California regarding the parish we started and built up in Encino. History often repeats itself, and we are all fragile human beings in the service of God and His people. No follower of Christ can avoid the Cross.

As part of the "re-founding," three new Friars from California, Fr. Christopher LaRocca, Fr. Jan Lundberg, and Fr. Juan Elias Medina, came to live the missionary life at Jinja in 2012. Fr. Juan Elias, young and enthusiastic and fitting in well in his new way of life on the mission, surprisingly returned to California after one year. Fr. Christopher and Fr. Jan was now the formation team at Duruelo. When Fr Christopher had to return to California for health reasons in 2017, Fr. Jan took over as Mission Superior with Fr. Peter Mary Vecellio as the latest recruit for the mission. Other members of the formation community are Bro. Andrew Bimpebwa, Fr. Augustine Sunday, Bro. Daudi Isabirye and Deacon Charles Okurie (he was ordained a priest in May 2019). Brother Emmanuel Mayinga is studying formation in Nairobi, and Fr. Godfrey Chandya Lega came to Arizona as Pastoral Vicar at Santa Cruz Carmelite parish in Tucson. Other friars at various stages of formation indicate that the mission is developing slowly but surely.

Another interesting development is the request by the Kenya region to send their postulants to Jinja for that stage of their formation. Welcoming them is a good sign of co-operation between the two areas, but it also brings up the urgency of another foundation. Early pastoral experience for the newly professed religious and appropriate Carmelite ministry outside of the formation work at Duruelo is of significant value for all.

In the recent Provincial Chapter (August 2020), Fr. Phillip Sullivan was appointed Mission Superior for Uganda. Some native-born Carmelites are now in essential formation positions, which is a further sign of the growth of the mission, with the native Carmelites stepping up to take greater responsibility. The current

American missionaries, Fr. Jan Lunberg – after ten years of service in Uganda – and Fr. Peter Mary Vecellio, returned to the States to take up the positions of Pastor in Stanwood, WA and local Superior at Mount Angel, OR. It is also good to know that other Friars from the American region have volunteered to go to the Mission "later on." Fr. Godfrey Chandya, who served at Santa Cruz parish in Tucson, AZ, has been transferred to St. Thérèse parish in Alhambra (Los Angeles) from where he will get more experience of "how things are done" in this part of the world and the Province.

In chapters 9 and 10, you will read the testimonies of missionaries and volunteers who have generously served the Uganda mission. As we give thanks for all those who have served and supported the Mission, we can fruitfully recall the words of St. Paul to the Corinthians:

> "What is Apollos, after all, and what is Paul? Ministers through whom you became believers, just as the Lord assigned each one. I planted, Apollos watered, **but only God caused the growth**. Therefore, neither the one who plants nor the one who waters is anything, but only God, who causes the growth." (I Cor. 3. 5-7).

May God's building, the Church in Uganda, be enriched by our Carmelite presence. May the people of Uganda come to know and appreciate our charism and, through it, find the richness of the Gospel of Jesus Christ, the Living Water of Life.

9
VOLUNTEERS and STAFF REMEMBER

"I give thanks to my God at every remembrance of you, praying always with joy in my every prayer for all of you, because of your partnership for the gospel from the first day until now." (Philippians 1.3-5)

St Paul had a great affection for the Christians of Philippi. That same gratitude and love are experienced over the years and in countless places, wherever the Gospel is preached and takes root. Priests and missionaries would never have done much without the brothers and sisters who prayed for them, cared for them, and supported them in many practical ways. In this chapter, we recall all those who helped our mission in Uganda; we give thanks for God's work in them and through them. Here are just a few of their stories:

HELGA NICE

Mission Office secretary, Helga Nice writes about "The most rewarding and meaningful job I ever had."

As I was grieving the passing of my dear husband - my best friend – and having retired from a 30 + year career in the financial services industry, my close connection with the Carmelites began. I was asked by Fr. Reginald McSweeney of the Carmelite House of Prayer and by Fr. David Costello to set up their accounting books. Fr Reginald was the new Prior of Oakville, and Fr David was beginning the Carmelite Mission in Uganda. They needed help in their respective offices to set up their accounting books. That was indeed a grace given to me by the Lord.

It was a great joy and truly a blessing to work daily for a few hours at the beautiful place of peace and serenity that both my husband and I loved and where we felt close to the Lord.

As a young student, my romantic girlhood dreams of going to Africa to help Dr. Albert Schweitzer soon met with stark reality as I received many reports, photos, and films from our missionaries in the field.

I learned that these beautiful, joyful people, especially in rural areas, live in abject poverty, in simple huts or lean-tos, sleeping on the bare earth with nothing but reed mats. They have no running water, no electricity, and their daily water supply is collected from open ponds of questionable purity. It is fetched mainly by women and children and must be transported long distances from the source to their humble abode. The heavy jerry cans are balanced very gracefully on their heads! Sadly, medical facilities are lacking, and families are constantly in danger of illness, especially Malaria. The children needed adequate schools, desks, and books, and sanitary facilities were also lacking. The local schools require a small fee for the children to attend. Often, the parents cannot afford these "school fees," so the children do not go to school at all.

For me, it was a great privilege to report on the progress of our missionaries: Fr. David Costello, Fr. Colm Stone, Lillian Kelly OCDS, and others. I published regular newsletters with many photographs and "Uganda Updates"; also sent e-mails sharing the news. Our missionaries worked long, arduous days to set up the rectory, renovate the church and bring the message of Jesus to the people. I felt truly inspired to share these reports and photographs with our many gracious, generous, and caring friends and supporters. The goodness and enthusiastic collaboration of our many loving benefactors touched me deeply. The number of these has continued to grow through the years – to this day.

Significantly, with the assistance of generous benefactors, they were able to drill wells to provide clean, healthful water and supply schools with proper desks for the children. Hundreds of sponsors stepped up to provide for their chosen child, to pay their school fees. These children sent lovely letters, expressing their gratitude. Many of the Churches in the outlying sub-parishes were renovated and rebuilt with direct gifts from individual donors. The joyful celebrations of Masses – most of which would last two hours or more – time seems irrelevant in Uganda – and other festivities and special occasions – Baptisms and Marriages, brought great joy to the people. In time a house for seminarians, "Duruelo," was built in Jinja near the source of the Nile for young Ugandans. And the work continues.

Thank you, Lord, for granting His grace to this one-time proud occupant of that coveted glass-enclosed corner office overlooking the San Francisco Bay. I have learned a lot – thank you, Lord, for this privilege of a lifetime and the best job I ever had.

—Helga Nice

BILL ZDANOSKI

As a Discalced Secular Carmelite, just recently retired (2020), I make this statement for Fr. David Costello OCD, a dear friend of mine and a former boss at the Mission Office of the Discalced Carmelite mission in Oakville. It is now eighteen years since the mission in Uganda began, and I worked as a secretary at this office, the U.S. contact for the venture, for about ten and a half years. The mission continues to flourish, with its central location now at Jinja, close to the banks of the Nile.

Bill and Brother Mark holding photos
of their sponsored children

I connected with the Mission Office when working one day a week, doing miscellaneous office work. When the prior secretary had resigned from her position, Fr David asked me if I would be willing to take over her job; my answer was a resounding "Yes." At that time, I was working for another employer but had no problem resigning from that position, as I always wanted to work for the Church and do some missionary work.

The inspiration to work at the Mission office came from my

constant desire to work where I could help others. Since for thirty-five years of my life, I was doing social work for the government, so after retiring, I wanted to continue to help others less fortunate than myself. At one time in my life, when I was in the 6th grade, I wanted to be a Priest or a Brother working somewhere in a mission situation. That never came to be, but when the opportunity came to work in the Mission Office, I considered it God's way of giving me another chance to do what I wanted to do, but differently and yet still in a missionary capacity. I was thrilled beyond words and still thank God for the great experience of working at the Carmelite mission office.

I have many special memories of working at the mission office. One of the most important was being part of the "Sponsor a Child" program. It was an opportunity to help a little boy or girl with their school tuition, daily lunch, and other family needs. It was so rewarding to watch these little ones grow and go through school to complete their education and then have a career, knowing that I have helped by being part of that process.

Other special memories were to see people getting clean water through our "Water Hope" project and how many were helped by getting water tanks and water filters. It was good to see the children progressing in their Catholic education and regular schooling. God bless all our missionaries for bringing home to all of us the missionary spirit of the Church. Thank God for allowing me to be part of that significant undertaking of the Carmelite mission.

—*Bill Zdanoski*

TOM and JEANETTE BENNETT

Tom and Jeanette Bennett

Our connection to the Uganda Carmelite mission started in 2006 when I taught 5th grade CCD (a Religious Education Program for all those children who attend non-Catholic schools) at St Apollinaris Parish in Napa. I was looking for a service project for my class, which would teach them to think of others and experience the wonderful feeling of helping those in need. Len Powers put me in touch with the Carmelite Mission office in Oakville.

When I talked to the children about helping the mission in Uganda, they were so excited they wanted to send toys and money. I explained that we couldn't send toys, so we came up with the idea of bringing in cans and bottles to recycle and sending the money to the mission. The Holy Spirit seemed to like our vision because it has grown to include the whole parish. It has been an excellent example for all the children and the parish. Receiving letters and photos from the mission, they see and enjoy the good fruit of their recycling efforts.

Since 2006 we have collected $23,000.00 in recycling money, all sorted and turned in to the mission office by my husband, Tom. The first two sponsored children have graduated from technical schools and now have jobs. The lunch program and the Little Flower School also benefit from this project.

The children of our parish know and experience that they can make a difference in the lives of the children of Uganda. Thanks be to God.

—Tom and Jeanette Bennett

LEN POWERS, OCDS
(Mission Director at St Apollinaris Parish, Napa, California)

On one warm and sunny morning, as I was leaving St. Apollinaris Church, Jeanette Bennett came sailing through the side door of the foyer. One could tell she was on a mission. Her face was bright and smiling and commanded my full attention. Jeanette was the teacher of the fifth-grade CCD. She knew I was involved with "The Faith in Action" volunteer group in the parish and asked if her students could help my group as part of their Lenten sacrifice of service.

My group does not take monetary assistance. I directed Jeanette to the Carmelite Mission office in Oakville, and she was happy to discover a suitable recipient for her students' desire for service. One of the main functions of the mission is to provide school fees and lunches for grade school children. Many of the parents could not afford either. As a result, the children's job potential was low or none due to a lack of education. In Uganda, the language of business is English. Without a good working knowledge of the English language, job opportunities are slim.

Stalwart Promoters of our Mission from St. Apollinaris Parish, Napa, California. Len Powers, Megan Gallagher, and Jeanette Bennett.

Jeanette outlined her plan of how the students could collect recyclables, bring them to class, and she would bring them home. Here, let the "St Joseph" of the process enter. Her husband, Tom, dutifully took on the work to complete Jeanette's plan of action. Tom separates the cans and the bottles, re-bags them, hauls the bags to the recycling center, where the attendant weighs them and pays Tom. Jeanette then forwards the money to the Carmelite Mission office at Oakville, a few miles north of Napa.

In 2017, the local Secular Carmelite community took on their recycling project modeled after Jeanette and Tom's venture. The Secular Order meets every 3rd Sunday at the Carmelite Monastery in Oakville. One of its members, their "Bottle and Can Man" (editor's note – that is Len Powers himself!), loads his pick-up and a small trailer with the bags brought there by the members. He then hauls the bags to his own house and follows the pattern set by Tom and Jeanette. The Secular Order started their project in 2017. Since then, the members have brought in over 6,000.00 (six thousand dollars) to educate and provide lunch for the children in the fifteen out-stations of St Kizito's Carmelite mission parish.

The memory of that meeting with Jeanette on that bright and sunny morning at St. Apollinaris remains as a lovely glow. Looking back, we can easily see that the Heavenly Father of the children in Uganda and us certainly had a hand in that meeting. Helping some of God's most loved people on earth, the poor and the children, is something that just screams out at us from the Scriptures. The children cannot thank us, so our compensation awaits us in heaven. We bring our baskets to heaven full of our good works for the poor and the children in Uganda. As Scripture constantly tells us, the givers are the receivers of God's love and blessings.

—*Len Powers*

CHERI KLUEVER, OCDS,
Volunteer, and Pilgrim

As a member of the Mary, Mother of the Church Secular Carmelite community in Oakville, California, knowledge of the Carmelite presence in Kenya and Uganda was readily available to me. After my retirement, I began volunteering weekly at the Oakville Carmelite Monastery in Oakville. There I learned more about the mission to Uganda and how a secular Carmelite friend from Sacramento, California, Lillian Kelly, had committed herself to stay in Uganda and help the people there. Admiring her generous spirit inspired me, but family commitments did not permit me to go on mission to Uganda. I helped out in the Mission office, writing thank you notes to benefactors, filing and sending letters from the school children to their sponsors, and mailing the Mission newsletters. That was Our Lord's way of giving me a chance to help out even though I could not go on mission. This work continued until I moved out of state in 2018.

So, you may ask, from where did this urge to go to the Mission come?. Growing up in Central San Joaquin Valley of California, I always looked forward to September. That was because I was eager to return to the new school year, but most of all, from the appreciation of smelling the sweet odor of grapes ripening on the vine and knowing that harvest was near. About this time every year, my mother would place a large cardboard box in the middle of the living room and remind my brother and me that it was time to fill it with toys and books we would share. She went through our clothing and picked out things we all had outgrown. After carefully washing and pressing the items, she placed them in the box. When the migrant families arrived, we gave them what we had gathered, including our mother's addition. These lessons of giving to others who had less were what I learned from an early age. It was natural for me to apply these lessons to the Carmelite mission. Seeing the pictures of the children from Uganda that came to the mission office in Oakville and noticing how little they had brought back memories of preparing those boxes for the migrant farm workers. It was time to sponsor a child. I selected a girl in middle school and continued her sponsorship until she graduated from college in Kampala.

In November 2011, it was a blessing for me to go on a pilgrimage to Uganda and see first-hand the children, the school, and living conditions. I saw a little boy carefully collecting soft drink bottle lids and making up a game with them, a far cry from American children's toys. I saw latrines at the schools instead of flushing toilets. I saw school rooms with dirt floors and roughly made long tables and benches instead of desks. I saw simple chalkboards instead of computers. Then I saw the smiling faces of children and heard their joyful singing. They had so little but reflected the face of Christ. Even nine years later, it's the sound of the children's laughter and singing that remains so vivid in my memory.

Although I no longer sponsor a child, I support young men training to be Carmelite priests and brothers to minister to their people. As Secular Carmelites, our apostolate is prayer and sharing the Teresian Carmelite spirituality. Still, we are members of the Church, and as such, we have the mission of sharing the Gospel throughout the world. "Whatever you did for one of these least brothers of mine, you did for me" (Matthew 25:40). That is what sustains my involvement.

—Cheri Kluever

TIM Mc CORMACK

My name is Tim Mc Cormack, and I come from Tipperary, Ireland. I am married to Norma, and we have four children, two boys and two girls, all redheads. I am a dairy farmer running the family farm. I worked for a pig farmer and wanted to take a break from my job and combine the holiday with doing some good.

Fr. David is my father's first cousin. As a child, I looked forward to his visits when he traveled home from Africa and America. I phoned him to see if I could help him in his mission in Uganda. The conversation confirmed my decision to go. While not sure how I could help, I had a strong desire to assist Fr. David and the local people he served. I left for Uganda in June 2003 for one year. At the start, I felt unsure of what I could do, but there were many roles that I fell into - painter, driver, farmer, builder, and I gave an occasional haircut.

Every morning started with Mass at 7 am before breakfast. The day's work started then. My main task was to develop the parish property to grow crops such as beans, pineapples, maize, etcetera to have food and income for the parish. Many Churches and schools were in sub-parishes in remote places. I frequently traveled to these sub-parishes with the mission priests.

Culturally, life was different than Ireland. Everybody had little and was grateful for any help given. Socially, I looked forward to "happy hour" celebrations for special occasions, such as birthdays, a new arrival to the mission, or a feast day. Occasionally, I would walk two miles to the trading center, Zigoti, to have a drink or two. I got to know Centurion, the shop owner, very well, and he "adopted" me into his tribe. He honored me with a tribal name, 'Nsereco.' All the other locals call me Mr. Tim. These formalities stopped when I returned home to my native Ireland.

At the end of the lane leading from the Mission Rectory lived a seven-year-old girl called Bridget with her family. She was unable to walk and, as such, could not attend school. I visited her a couple of times a week and became attached to her. While visiting, we used her walker to get her mobile again. I also have strong memories of bringing a woman, the wife of one of the parish catechists, from the hospital in Mityana to her home. She had recently delivered a little boy, whom Fr. Colm baptized ("the tiniest baby I ever saw" – Fr. Colm) and was named Elizabeth. The mother's prognosis was poor due to the presence of HIV. I carried her into her home and felt completely helpless as there was nothing more I could do; she was in great distress. The following morning news came that she had passed away—a sad ending for a beautiful young woman.

The children in the schools were happy, even if many had to walk a long distance to get there. Visiting the schools, the children would always entertain us with singing and dancing. I also remember a local lady who attended Mass every morning. Somebody told us that she was sleeping underneath rusty steel sheeting; we arranged to build a small house with one room for her. She required a lot of convincing that she was worthy of it but eventually moved in. My overriding memory from Uganda is the generosity and hard work of the priests and sisters from the Carmelite order. Their efforts to educate, feed and nourish the people spiritually largely go unnoticed outside their religious order.

I still look forward to visits and calls with Fr David. We fondly remember him in our home, and my older son is called Daithi, which is the Irish language version for David. We named him Daithi after his grandfather (Davy) and Fr. David. I can only hope he shows half the qualities of both in the coming years.

—*Tim McCormack*

THERESA THOMAS, OCDS

My name is Theresa Thomas; I've been a secular member of the Discalced Carmelites since my first meeting in 1992. I volunteered at the Carmelite House of Prayer, where the Mission Office is headquartered, for twelve years, from 2007 through 2019. I helped with mailings and general office work for the mission as needed. Other volunteer work included scrubbing floors and window cleaning, refinishing furniture, making and mending habits and liturgical vestments, and laundering altar linens.

In 2009, I visited Uganda as part of Fr David's second "Mission Awareness Pilgrimage." There are so many memories! The red clay soil, so like the red clay soil in Alabama where my grandparents lived, and the shacks along the deeply rutted dirt roads that were so like the shacks I saw as a child in Alabama. It was impossible not to connect life in Uganda with blacks and poor whites in the Deep South. We visited two sub-parishes, where crowds of children greeted us and later performed for us, and where we received a detailed report on what they have accomplished and what their current needs were – hoping, of course, for more funds. There was a simplicity and directness that was refreshing. And the liturgies!

The people danced up the aisles of the open-air worship spaces with their offerings of chickens, fruit, and vegetables. We did some touristy things, too, visiting the Equator, the source of the Nile in Lake Victoria, and taking in the natural beauty of Uganda. In Jinja, we saw the newly built House of Studies and enjoyed a pot-luck barbecue of goat cooked under the soil – delicious. In Kampala, there was the Basilica - no, it must have been the Cathedral – where our guide stated, "we steal things here, so …" (It was a shock to hear that casual statement of reality). We also saw the urban sprawl and the squalor that spoke volumes about poverty and the difference between rich and poor, how few material goods are needed to be rich, and how little we appreciate the blessings of the material riches we enjoy.

One thing always leads to another in life, which has been especially true regarding the mission. Sister Antonia, who organized and accompanied us on our adventures, was impressive in her knowledge, energy, and generosity in serving the people of the parish – a genuinely saintly person without any pretension. Later, when she came to the States, I had the privilege of lending her my Carmelite brown down jacket because it was December and cold, and she didn't have the proper clothing. I still have the jacket, and every time I put it on, I still think of her and feel the grace and love she left me in it. While we were in Uganda, she taught our little group the "Glory be" in Luganda. I recorded her angelic voice singing it on my phone to learn it myself, and I still play it from time to time, separated by time and distance but still joining her in prayer. Isn't that one of the most beautiful mysteries of God? I wish I could play it for you now.

When I started the pilgrimage, I understood it to be a way to increase public awareness and financial support of the Order's work in Uganda and the very needs that exist there. By the time I had returned home, I did have a better understanding of the conditions in Africa. But more importantly, I had a much keener appreciation of my own mission in life to overcome discrimination and promote a fuller, complete understanding of who GOD is so that meaningful participation in the life of the Church could be available to ALL and especially to women. As I came home from the airport, I listened to an NPR radio program about how the economics of poverty drove women fishmongers (most fishmongers there are women) to trade sexual favors for fish from the fishers along the shores of Lake Victoria. That contributed to the rampant spread of AIDS in Uganda and Kenya. The women have little choice; they must put out for the men if they want fish to sell. The fishermen, when interviewed, expressed pride in knowing the importance of getting tested often but said nothing about changing their conduct. How appalling! "How does getting tested help you avoid contracting AIDS"? I wondered. Now, during the coronavirus pandemic, I see the same ignorance operating in this country in the White House, where people have said, "We were getting tested so often, I thought we would be safe."

These are the things that have inspired me and sustained me through all the difficulties of life; the memories, the experiences, the connections, and the love between people across time and space, because they make it so clear that we are much more like one another than we are different. We have the same hopes, the same fears, the same joys, and the same sorrows. We are all one in God.

—*Theresa Thomas*

MEGHAN GALLAGHER

When I was eight years old, I was first introduced to the Carmelite mission in Uganda. I was a second-grade student, sitting in the pews of St Apollinaris parish in Napa, California, on a Tuesday afternoon when I heard Father David talk about the mission and the students and families they served. Father David specifically spoke about the students who sat on rocks around a tree since there weren't enough classrooms. That was mind-blowing for me. How could I learn in a school classroom with plenty of books and school supplies, and these students did not even have a classroom? It just wasn't fair. I was stunned. Upset. Even angry and motivated to do something about it.

It is no exaggeration to say that afternoon changed my life. I went home, found an empty water jug, and immediately began collecting small change. I rummaged through my room and gathered school supplies, clothes, and books, and shipped the entire lumpy, oversized box to Uganda. My family signed up to sponsor three children, supporting them for school fees and other expenses that came up. From then on, my involvement in the Carmelite Mission became an essential and intensely personal part of my life.

Twelve years later, in college, I finally had the opportunity to visit Kyengeza. I spent five weeks living with Sr. Antonia and the rest of the Sisters of Mount Carmel, helping in the primary school, tutoring at the special needs home, and just being part of the community there. One of the primary school teachers happened to be on leave while I was there. I spoke no Luganda, and my eighteen or so five-year-old students spoke little English. But through lots of hand signals and drawings, we fumbled through it together. In the afternoons, I usually walked down the hill to the home where several 'special needs' students lived. I would spend the afternoons helping with homework assignments, reading, or simply playing outside. Then I looked forward to dinners with Sr. Antonia, Sr. Grace, Sr. Edith, and others. My room was next to the chapel, and every morning I woke up to their morning Mass and singing. Trinity, the cat, was a permanent fixture on the sun-soaked veranda.

My most profound memory from the mission was visiting the families that my own family had sponsored for almost ten years. I had grown up with these students and their families in some ways. We received multiple letters throughout the year, each filled with updates on school, their families, and special events in their lives. It was an incredible experience to meet each student and see the home and community in which they grew up. Each family welcomed me into their home, offering bountiful food and a few live chickens as gifts. However, we couldn't say much with the language barrier; not much needed to be said. I felt I had learned as much from them and our exchange of letters as they did from our contributions to their school fees.

Sr. Grace had also identified several families that were particularly struggling. She made it a point to go out and visit them, often walking long distances to visit each home. One Saturday, Sister took me with her. She would sit and listen as they talked about whatever struggles they were going through. She offered community, companionship, and the knowledge that someone cared for them and prayed for them. Being present with them in their struggles and their journey was profoundly moving, and it continues to inspire me.

I am now 27 years old, and that same jug sits in my bedroom. I've since graduated from the University of Notre Dame with a degree in International Development studies and now live in Washington D.C. I've traveled to 18 countries in Africa, working on U.S. foreign aid programs to sub-Saharan Africa as my career. That Tuesday afternoon in St Apollinaris parish, 20 years ago, and that summer in Kyengeza, profoundly changed my life.

—Meghan Gallagher

SARAH KATE

(a native of Uganda, living and working in the U.S. for 25 years)

Sarah Kate with Fr. Christopher and student

On February 18, 2014. 11:00 pm, I stepped out of the Sabina Airlines flight onto the rough asphalt ground at Entebbe Airport, Uganda. I was one of the 5 USA missionaries of the "Mission Awareness Pilgrimage" to the Carmelite Mission in Uganda. The others had arrived a day earlier. The airport seemed smaller than I remember. When I left 20 years ago, there was political turmoil with many Army personnel at the airport. My anxiety was soon replaced by excitement and delight when I saw the Carmelite driver hold up a WELCOME sign with my name on it, courtesy of Fr. David and Sr. Antonia Dulong. They arranged all our local travel and lodging.

Off we went to Kyengeza near Mityana. At the convent, the amazing Sister Antonia welcomed me. I soon realized that this young, calm, sweet, smiling sister was a pillar of strength and love. She was born and raised in France, entered the Carmelites in Austria, served nine years in Uganda, and spoke fluent Luganda (Uganda's commonest dialect). We joined the other pilgrims, Diana from New Mexico, Kyoshi, Opal, and Fr. David from California. For the next four days, we experienced first-hand the Lord's amazing grace, channeled through Carmelite Fathers, Brothers and Sisters, with the help of St. Therese of the Child Jesus, Patroness of the Missions. They serve Ugandans generously to provide spiritual and material development, with the funds and generosity of the many USA and European benefactors. We started each day with Mass celebrated by Fr David.

We visited several projects managed and coordinated by Sr. Antonia and her staff – Sharon Najjengo, Annette, Sr. Margret, and Fr. Francis. We received a rousing welcome from the St. Ambrose High School students at Kyengeza. We spent time at several Primary schools and experienced their lunch programs where the children are provided with posho (corn meal) and beans, resulting in improved grades and fewer dropouts. That program is an additional one to the sponsorship program, and the children, as well as the teachers, greatly appreciate it. The children provided us with cultural dancing and singing in a lively style. The visit to the St Theresa's Home for the 'special needs children' was particularly moving and touching. The star of the visit was little three-year-old Daniela, sponsored by one of our Pilgrims, Diana. When Diana herself died not long after her Uganda pilgrimage, her husband continued the sponsorship of little Daniela, so loved by his now-deceased wife.

After a scary ride on an uneven dirt road, we made it to Bukalagi HIV clinic and maternity home. It is partially funded by the mission and co-managed by Sr. Antonia and her team. We met the medical staff, who gave us a tour of the facility, wards, pharmacy, and HIV drugs stock. I noticed they use a "charcoal stove" to boil water in the labor ward!!! No electric/gas stoves or water heater – things we take for granted here in the USA.

Lack of clean water is a significant problem in Uganda. For any American, it is unimaginable, yet for the Ugandan rural majority, the only water source is a dirty, mosquito-infested pond often miles away from home. I was delighted to see a Borehole, donated by the "Water Hope" foundation in California, pumped water from its deep source. Girls line up and fill their 20-liter jerrycans and head-carry them home two or three miles away. A few lucky locals have been blessed with Crest tanks to harvest rainwater, also donated by USA benefactors.

The big missionary project of the Pilgrimage was the training and distribution of water filters for a group of parents of young children. Its spiritual base was St. Teresa's love for the story of the Samaritan woman's encounter with Jesus. Fr. David brought 50 water filters with him to provide for families of young children. In the training session, we showed them how to assemble the filtering systems, trained the participants on their use, and gave them an appreciation of "The Water of Life" story from the Gospel. Since I can speak the local language, I helped with the training and was privileged to be an interpreter for my fellow pilgrims. It was humbling and rewarding to see the delighted recipients with happy smiles of gratitude for the special equipment to give their children and families clean water.

The highlight was when we met the Kyengeza High School students. Many of them have sponsors among the much younger USA students, such as those from St. Apollinaris Primary school, Napa, and the CCD (i.e., religious education) students of the same parish through their recycling program for Uganda. They filed up smartly dressed in white shirts and socks and navy-blue uniforms; each received a personal, handwritten message from their sponsor, hand-delivered by Fr. David. They were thrilled, and the smiles all around inspired me. That's love! You are never too young or too old to be a missionary disciple of Jesus with smiles.

On the way to Namugongo, the National Shrine of the Ugandan Martyrs, I invited my pilgrim mates to my parents' house for a traditional Ugandan meal. We had delicacies of Matooke (cooked bananas), chicken Oluwombo (steamed casserole made with banana leaves), ground Peanut sauce, Chapatis, Posho, freshly squeezed fruit juices, and fresh organic fruits for dessert. Everyone enjoyed this Ugandan culinary experience. We visited the Nuns at Kiyinda, the Conference center at Mizigo, and finally the Carmelite House for students, "Duruelo" at Jinja. We met Fr. Christopher and Fr. Jan, and the students training to become Carmelite priests and brothers.

The devotion and commitment of our Priests and Sisters who leave their comfortable homes in America and in Europe to serve the poor people of Africa is a beautiful inspiration. They dispensed love, hugs, smiles, humor, support, strength, responsibility, kindness, and more love. They seemed to know each one by name. Thank you for all the love and for enriching the Catholic Church and the country of Uganda; God bless you all, priests, sisters, and nuns. All the programs financed by donors to help the young and the elderly of Uganda are a true blessing. Thank you, friends and benefactors, for planting seeds of clean water and education to develop the country and spread God's love.

As a USA citizen with Ugandan heritage, I am abundantly blessed. I am also greatly challenged to do more for the underprivileged in my own country of Uganda.

—*Sarah Kate*

LEYLA NAJARI

(As a seventeen-year-old High School senior, Leyla volunteered for our mission in Uganda in 2019)

Saying goodbye to my family and home in Tucson, Arizona, I headed off for the adventure of a lifetime. Looking at my ticket, which read 'Final destination, Uganda: flight time, 26 hours', my stomach filled up with fear and anxiety. I felt as if I would throw up, but I knew I had to do this. Since I was little, I have always wanted to volunteer in Africa. I had heard stories of the suffering and hardship the people experience there, and I wanted to make a difference.

When I arrived at the St. Theresa's Home for special needs children, directed by Sr. Antonia, a Carmelite Sister, I was tired and relieved and was looking forward to working with the children. That is where I was to spend most of my time in Uganda. I lived the way the children lived, ate what they ate, and slept where they slept. There was no expectation that I would receive any special treatment because I was American. On the contrary, now residing in their country, I needed to assimilate their ways. My lifestyle completely shifted from one end to the other. I dug holes in the garden to plant cassava plants and beans. I was to survive on these vegetables for the next few months.

The next skill I had to acquire was cooking by fire. First, I gathered enough dry wood. Then, I built a pit big enough to light a fire. I then put the pieces of wood in the hole. I wrapped plastic around a stick, then lit the plastic with a match, and then threw it into the pit. Day by day, I repeated this process. By the end of a long day's work, I stared at my dirty hands covered with the land's soil and felt an air of pride. I never imagined that I would ever use my hands for work of this kind. I lived with the children who were forgotten or abandoned - stripped of their rights and suffering greatly, in conditions beyond what anyone in the United States could imagine. Yet, they are still able to love and be loved. Just showing them that someone cared for them was so important to them, and I am so grateful that I was part of helping them realize their self-worth. I challenge everyone to be thankful for what they have instead of wishing for more. These people have nothing, and yet they are still overflowing with joy. Everyone can help, capable of showing kindness and compassion. We can all make the difference we want to see in the world, and we must do it. I pray that I could make a difference in just one of their lives because they have forever changed mine.

Deo was one of the children I worked with every day. He suffered from contractions of the Tendo Achilles, which is common for people with autism. This condition prevented him from being able to walk without assistance. Although he was physically impaired, his eyes lit with joy as he played and learned with the other children. He loved to play with them yet faced adversity and challenges while playing. Still, his little heart enjoyed every moment of it. Although he seemed different on the outside, he was still a child on the inside.

However, since Deo's autism was severe, he could not go to school at the orphanage. While he did attend a school for disabled children, he soon left because his condition was not extreme enough. Deo was stuck; he was in a place where he could not receive help because he was either too disabled or not disabled enough. That is where I came in. My job was to prepare Deo for school and work with him in physical therapy, speech therapy, and eye coordination. Every day we focused for 20 minutes on tracing. He traced letters and numbers and worked on spelling his name. You could see the fire and determination in his eyes because he was allowed to learn and grow. In one month, with the help he received in this therapy, he could return to the school at the orphanage.

The difference between Deo and the other children at the orphanage was that he was born into a wealthy family. Yet his father was ashamed of his disabilities. Therefore, he chose to abandon him instead. He left Deo on his own accord under the care of his grandmother. Unfortunately, she physically abused him. She would push him on the floor to remain on top of his elbows and knees for long periods. As a result, he formed calcium deposits. He had two masses protruding from below his skin on both sides of his knees and elbows. On several occasions, he suffered beatings to the point where he was left unconscious. His father had the resources to help him at a young age, but he hid his son from society and left him to face the world alone. His past taught me how to live my future. I learned how to be grateful for the gift of life, and I also knew how weak and selfish people could be. We take simple things for granted, such as walking, talking, eating, and drinking fresh water. In the United States, we have access to all our essential needs, even if we are poor and homeless. The homeless in America are more prosperous than most people in Uganda.

By the time a month had passed, Deo had grown exponentially. He was able to walk correctly without the assistance of a helping hand. A significant accomplishment for him was using the restroom without help, meaning that he could now hold and aim properly. He developed the necessary skills to achieve these tasks through hard work, perseverance, and an indomitable will. It shows that although this was done in a short period, anyone can overcome their limitations with enough support and love. I did not give up on him, and I would not let him give up either. It was frustrating at times, and I felt hopeless. I realized that simple tasks that seemed essential proved significant milestones to him. But through our joined efforts to improve his mental and physical condition, we both witnessed a radical change. Unlike his father, I cared for him, worked with his disabilities, and taught him that there was nothing to be ashamed of. Even though he seemed different from other kids, he was not.

Deo was just one of the many children I worked with in Uganda, but he has inspired me to continue my volunteer work in foreign countries. I would like to return to Uganda and witness

Deo's progress now that he can return to school. I am also considering traveling to other parts of Africa and helping those who need medical attention and encouragement. I hope that I will inspire others to follow my example because the need is great, and we can only help others when we can break out of our selfishness.

—Leyla Najari

MERLIE PABLICO, OCDS
(St. Elijah Community, Berkeley, California)

In 2017, the intervention of St. Therese of the Child Jesus, Co-Patroness of the missions, sent a strong sense of purpose to my Carmelite vocation. Our Carmelite mission was the heart of my trip to Uganda, which deeply moved me, but the fruit of my first visit and the principal benefit was – indescribable joy! Fr. Fred, a native of Uganda, and some Carmelite Friars were my connections for this trip. July the 3rd was my first stop – at St. Ursula School for Mentally Challenged Children. From the moment I got out of the car, dozens of kids came running to me to give me a great welcome, jumping up and down, hugging my legs, shaking my hands, touching my face and hair, and just giggling with joy. I was overwhelmed by their physical affection. It was like two worlds colliding across the ocean in one challenging yet beautiful human family.

On July the 10th, Fr. Peter gave me a ride to Kyengeza, where I met Sister Antonia for the first time. The following day, she brought me to the St. Therese Little Flower school, one of the mission's achievements from Fr. David's time. Sr. Antonia put me into one of the classrooms to sub for one of the sick teachers. Amazingly, the children were incredibly communicative with an impressive command of the English language.

These experiences made me proud to be a Secular Carmelite, and I grew in faith by serving these vulnerable children. My efforts were showered fruitfully by the Holy Spirit. I am confident that my purpose of being a Carmelite became more apparent for me. My whole mission trip was a life-changing experience that broadened my spirituality and inspired me to a life of service and volunteerism. However, the overriding force that drives me is faith.

Cooking dinner and feeding these vulnerable children, being there to serve, was uniquely punctilious to my experience. No less important was joining the Sisters for Mass at 5:00 am, Evening Prayer at 6:00 pm, Adoration of the Blessed Sacrament, celebrating the feast of Our Lady of Mount Carmel, and meeting the Carmelite Nuns at their monastery in Mityana was a further blessing. These are just a few of my memories of a memorable visit to Uganda.

—*Merlie Pablico*

OTHER VOLUNTEERS

We need to recognize and pay tribute to other lay volunteers who served generously at our Mission at Kyengeza - Bert Wooning from Napa, California, John Slater (deceased) from St Helena, California, Ellen Petit from Michigan, and Melanie Heard from South Dakota.

Our Parish School of St. Kizito was also the designated location for two Peace Corps volunteers, Lynn McDermott from Massachusetts and Gloria Reichman from Washington state. Lynn was a young Peace Corps volunteer whose mother addressed letters and packages to "Sister Lynn" at our parish address. Her mother felt that the additional title of "Sister" would guarantee the safe arrival of the goods to her daughter. Lynn was not particularly religious, but she fitted in well in our Catholic school and parish. Gloria was considerably older for a Peace Corps volunteer but not old enough to be called "Jaja." Instead, the school children, who loved her library classes, affectionately called her "Aunt Gloria." God bless each one of them, and God rest John Slater.

10

FRIARS and MISSIONARIES REMEMBER

Chapter 10 deals with the memories of the missionaries who served or are still serving in Uganda and the native-born Ugandan Carmelites. They are developing the initial efforts of the earlier missionaries to share the Carmelite charism with their people and with the Church in Uganda. We begin with Fr Colm Stone, who passed on to his eternal reward in 2019. May the Lord reward him abundantly for his unique part for four years at our mission. Fr Colm sent many "Updates" back to the Mission office in Oakville, Calif. Here are two of them, the first from his experience at Ttumbu sub-parish and the second from Mount Angel, Oregon, where he served on his return to the States. The second Update we will hold until the end of this chapter.

FR COLM STONE, OCD

Fr. Colm Stone

"The Wedding Feast of Ttumbu"
(Uganda Update of Oct. 15, 2004)

To describe a big celebration here in Uganda is like trying to explain the Grand Canyon; you must be there in person, and even then, you realize that there is more happening than can be expressed in words. The wedding feast at Ttumbu was that kind of an experience for me (Fr Colm). It was unusual that one couple was getting married, and in the same Mass, the father and mother of the groom were celebrating their 50th wedding anniversary. The Bishop was the principal celebrant.

The beautiful harmony and rhythms of the choir were striking; they swayed in unison as if they were one person. They enjoyed themselves as they responded to the conductor maintaining the beat with graceful and rhythmic gestures that were a pleasure to watch. Five drummers complemented the choir, acting like a heartbeat and drawing the whole assembly into the song.

Liturgical dance has not taken hold much in the Western world. But here in Africa, it would be unthinkable not to have dancers at a big occasion. To the accompaniment of the choir and drums, the dancers – regularly children in festive costumes – move in unison with graceful hand gestures that radiate great energy and joy. They lead the procession of whatever is being honored – the celebrant at the entrance, the book of the Gospels. The bride and groom and the jubilarians, led by the dancers, carried the offertory gifts in procession. When entering into such a joyful celebration, you lose all sense of time. So, I was amazed to find that four hours passed from the entrance song to the final blessing at the end of Mass. At this stage, things were only getting underway. There was a short break before the entertainment began and another hour and a half before the meal began. You wouldn't want to be in a hurry to go anywhere. I felt privileged to be there and wondered to myself, "how am I going to share this with the folks back home"?

I had planned to walk home from the wedding, so I did, leaving my habit and Mass vestments with Fr David to take home in the truck. The way home was a dirt path and mostly downhill. I heard a bicycle behind me at one stage and stepped off the trail to let the man pass. He stopped and greeted me and offered me a ride on the back carrier. Knowing the terrain, I thanked him but said I would prefer to walk. At that, he got down from the bike and proceeded to accompany me on foot until we reached his destination. He walked beside me when the path was wide enough and behind me when it was too narrow for both of us. My Luganda is not too great, and his English wasn't perfect, but between the two of us, we managed to get along fine, chatting away and being "of one heart if not always of one mind" as we journeyed towards home. This "accompanying of visitors" seems to be a part of the African culture because it has happened to me several times, and it's always a pleasant surprise. The Ugandan tradition of warm hospitality finds expression in many lovely ways.

After our evening meal every day, our community remembers all of you in our prayer. May God continue to bless you with the peace and joy of Christ.

—*Fr. Colm Stone*

Fr. Colm with his confreres and friends celebrating the
40th anniversary of his Profession.

FR STEPHEN WATSON, OCD

The Sacrifice of the Mass is a memorial, the remembrance, of Our Lord's blessed Passion, Resurrection, and Ascension into heaven. "Do this in memory of me," says the Lord. Memory plays an integral part in our spiritual journey to union with God.

It seems necessary to remember at a time when people are so forgetful, and intentionally so, of the good things God has done in us, through us, and for us. I am personally grateful that Fr. David has collected and preserved memories of the beginnings and the progress of the mission of California-Arizona Province of Discalced Carmelites in Uganda. His 'African Memories' is part chronicle, part memoir, and part reflection on the nature of the Christian mission in the light of the Second Vatican Council.

Fr. Stephen Watson

In the first chapter of *'African Memories'* Fr David writes that the intro to Uganda was the Superior General's invitation in 1993 to the three American provinces to take charge of a recently established International House of Formation in Nairobi. In November 1998, Definitor General, Fr. Jeremiah Fitzpatrick, made a fraternal visit to our province. The Superior General sent him to ask us to take on a mission to Uganda. He called all the friars to El Carmelo Retreat House in Redlands in southern California. Fr. Gerald Werner was our Provincial, and he and the Provincial Council took Fr. Jeremiah's request seriously, as indeed it was. The Provincial Chapter of May 1999 discussed the matter further and decided to undertake the mission to Uganda.

In February 2002, I drove Fr. David from the Oakville Monastery to the San Francisco International Airport. In October, as the newly elected Provincial for a second term, I went to Uganda to accept the administration of the Parish of St. Kizito in Kyengeza. It was Mission Sunday. God's loving Providence was manifest.

This photo shows Fr. Stephen on the river Nile

The country of Uganda was developing at such a pace that each time I visited, there were new roads, buildings, and commercial endeavors. Our Mission was also growing. I am proud of our Province and its commitment to developing the Discalced Carmelite Order in Uganda for Uganda and the Church. I often had some Ugandans say, "I am proud of you, Father." It was their way of saying they were happy with something you had done for them. And if you complimented a Ugandan on their work, you were likely to get the reply, "Thank you for appreciating." I hope and pray for the day when the Discalced Carmelite Friars of Uganda will take control of their destiny under the guidance of the Holy Spirit.

St Teresa had a heroic zeal for "the salvation of souls." This zeal made her do all in her power to help the missionary work of evangelization. In her Exclamations (outpourings of her heart after receiving Holy Communion), she cries out:

"…..During this mortal life, all worldly delights are uncertain, even though they seem to come from Thee, unless the love of our neighbor bears them company. Who loves not his brethren, loves not Thee, my Lord, for Thy blood, shed for us, bears witness to Thy boundless love for the sons of Adam."

Fr Jerome Gracian expressed the same sentiment in a letter to Francisco del Nino Jesus, who was trying to decide on joining the Discalced Carmelites. Gracian says," Christ left such a good monastery as heaven and such a good cell as the heart of His Father to die for us."

Such was the zeal of the Discalced Carmelites that they would even leave their monasteries to go to Africa.

—Fr. Stephen Watson

SISTER ANTONIA DULONG

Hello! I'm Sr. Antonia, a member of the Sisters of Mary of Mount Carmel, born in France but working in Austria. I was attracted to the Sisters and joined their congregation. My journey to Uganda began on the 24th of July 2002 and since then I am journeying in faith with marvelous people. 19 years, full of surprises and challenges, some good, some less joyful, some difficulties, and here I am still struggling and behold … still full of hope and love.

When our congregation decided to start a mission in Uganda, I was one of only three volunteers. My motivation was simple; as a disciple of Jesus, vowed to His service, it was evident that I had to be ready, wherever and whenever the community was in need. As well as that, I sometimes felt I needed a change from my comfortable life as a religious nurse and from an established institution and a familiar environment. I had no clue what would come and what I would do. I jumped into the water with the certainty that God gave me the gift of knowing how to swim, and with the assurance of His help, I would reach where He wanted me to go and do what He wanted me to do.

Leaving my home in Europe and my sisters in the community was difficult, but the phrase that gave me courage was "No turning back, no turning back"! I had chosen these words and those of St. Paul at my profession ceremony "Forgetting all that lies behind me and straining forward to what lies in front, I am racing towards the finishing point to win the prize of God's heavenly call in Christ Jesus" (Phil. 3,13). They inspired and sustained me.

The journey with my companion missionary, Sr. Elizabeth, was long and thoughtful, but eventually, we touched down softly on Ugandan land at Entebbe airport. My first impression on leaving the airline was like entering a sauna; it was humid and hot. Fr Dennis Kyemwa warmly welcomed us and took good care of us by providing overnight rest and bringing us to Mityana the next day.

We spent our first month at the Carmelite Monastery, "Queen of Martyrs," in Mityana. Our stay at the monastery was a time of adaptation, learning the language, getting oriented in the country, and deciding on a parish to set up our convent. In Europe, I considered myself easily adaptable to new situations, but it took me a whole month in Uganda to feel free and comfortable with people and with a new place. Every evening from 6 pm until supper time at 7 pm, I would walk up and down in the garden attached to the monastery, trying to memorize the "Our Father" and "Hail Mary" in Luganda. I only managed to recite these prayers freely when I started praying with the children at Kyengeza. God was telling me that what we had planned would not be easy. But it would require lots of patience, endurance, and courage – a challenging task for me who, by nature, am full of ideas and want to realize them as soon as possible and at the same time!

Our life at Kyengeza was simple - no electricity, no hot water, basic food. We used to pray on the veranda (because the Church was too dark) facing the hill of Ttumbu, which we called our Mount Carmel, reminding us of the place of our origins in Israel. It was a quiet and meditative time, and many times we were joined by other living creatures - a goat, the hens, and the duck; did they want to participate in our prayer, or did they just like being with human beings? By 7 pm, it was dark, and after supper, the only thing you could do was to pray and go to bed and wake up refreshed at the sound of the cock crowing and inviting us to another new day of surprises.

I especially like to remember the time spent with handicapped children with special needs. I visited them regularly depending on their needs. One day visiting a group in Kabule sub-parish, I spent much time reviewing each child and encouraging the parents to continue with the prescribed exercises. It was getting late, and I knew I had to leave, but they insisted on eating something or at least taking something home. I got five small eggs from a grateful mother to bring home and share with my Sisters in the community. They insisted that I take them. Another time I was given a boiled egg with a coca-cola, a food combination that I had never experienced, but they were so happy to have something to share I had to take it and eat it; it was delicious!

Another event I like to recall was when I received my Luganda name when I started working at the St. Francis Hosfa Clinic. The nurse welcomed me in a lovely way; it was the very first time we met, and she announced, "From now on, you are my daughter. You are NANTONGO." She continued to call me by that name, and so did the others. I felt at home even though I struggled a lot with the local language and English too, and besides that, I did not know much about tropical diseases. I found myself "back at school" as I had to ask about lots of things.

The most difficult challenge was understanding the people of another culture and their way of expressing themselves about their sickness. I learned a lot also at the St Jacinta clinic in Zigoti, even about eating the locally prepared dishes like the unique "Fish Head" dish with the big eyes looking at me. The nurses enjoyed giving me these dishes to see how I would react. I also began to understand what it meant to have a "missionary stomach" as I tried not to disappoint them!

These are some of my memories. There are many others I could recall, but I have written more than the requested one page, so I think I better stop! In conclusion, I can say a beginning is not easy, but with God's grace and strength, everything is possible. We are only tools in the hands of God. The most important thing is acknowledging it and letting oneself be at His purpose.

—*Sr. Antonia Dulong*

LILLIAN KELLY, OCDS

Lillian was the surprise member of our little founding band of missionaries to Uganda. Yet, she was accepted and respected because she was a Secular Carmelite and because of her previous lay missionary experience in Nepal as a public health nurse. Lillian had a fruitful stay in Uganda for four years serving at the Mission, especially with the parish's youth, the Xaverians, and the Secular Carmelite group. Also, she served generously and courageously in the Diocesan Health Office. At present, because of poor health, she would be unable to write any of her memories. However, I have a short letter she wrote to me before the 2016 OCDS Congress, held at San José and attended by over 500

OCDS. Also present at that Congress were: Fr. Godfrey Chandya Lega, Brother Andrew Bimpebwa, and Vivian Nabule OCDS, all three native Ugandan Carmelites. The theme of the Congress was "Bringing God into the world by our Secular Carmelite Missionaries." Here is a copy of her letter.

Lillian with Fr. Stephen

Dear Fr. David,
Congratulations on the fruit of your vision for the Mission of the Discalced 2002. During the Congress, June 23 to June 26, 2016, I know the JOY will be great – overflowing and without measure!

For myself, the Mission was everything I ever wanted to do as a nurse, and God placed my desire within the Secular Carmelite vocation.

Forever grateful, with fond enduring memories,

—Nasanza – Lillian (Elephant clan)

FR. CHRISTOPHER LAROCCA, OCD

Jambo! (Greetings). Katonda weebale! (Thanks be to God, the Creator), and thanks to Fr. David for giving me and others this opportunity to reminisce about the blessings we received as missionaries in Africa.

The name of the young altar server I met in Ekpoma, Nigeria, at our Carmelite parish of Mary the Queen, comes to mind - "God's Time"; yes, his name was "God's Time"! When the priest inscribes and blesses the Easter Candle at the Easter Vigil liturgy, he says, "Jesus Christ, the Alpha and Omega, all time belongs to Him." My time as a missionary – 'once a missionary, always a missionary' – continues to be a time of God's blessings and graces; it is indeed God's time.

I was born in Mission City, San Francisco, assumed to be a missionary. Since childhood, I participated in the Holy Childhood Association, a branch of the Congregation of the Propagation of the Faith, at my Parochial School of St. Veronica. We would raise money for poor children in Africa and receive word of their Baptism. Africa is close in a child's imagination, and poor children are our friends. My mother regularly donated to the Propagation of the Faith, and at a certain point, she presented me! As a young Carmelite Brother, I studied for two years at the Pontifical University, Urbaniarum, run by Propaganda Fidei, now known as the Sacred Congregation for the Evangelization of Peoples. In that "Missionary Environment," I was formed by friendship and scholarship to evangelize, to be a missionary. "Go and Teach," the motto of the University, is based on the missionary mandate at the end of Matthew's Gospel -"Go out to all the nations and teach them, baptizing them ..." This same little yet powerful word "GO," is used at the end of every Mass to send all forth as missionaries and evangelizers. Go on glorifying God by your lives.

In August 1999, I arrived in Africa for the first time at Nairobi, Kenya, where I met with Fr. David. I had hoped to join him but was named Master of novices in our home region of the Province. However, 'Patience obtains all'! In May 2012, I arrived in Uganda as a part of a new team to "refound the mission with an emphasis on formation." Sadly, we had to leave our parish of St Kizito at Kyengeza (from which reality we have not entirely recovered). The "God's Time" experience, of my labors of love in Africa, from May 2012 to October 2017, is beyond words. Due to some health issues, I had to return to California. Since then, I have been assigned as Mission Zelator, raising awareness and financial support for our mission in Uganda. I am forever blessed and grateful to my Carmelite family and my brothers and sisters in Africa.

As a memorable highlight and unique event, I will mention the visit of the Holy Father, Pope Francis, to Namugomgo on November 29th, 2015, for the Golden Jubilee of the Canonization of the 22 Ugandan Martyrs. What a celebration! The theme of the Jubilee was from Acts, Chapter 1, "You will be my witnesses."

Yes, God's Time! Go out 'ad gentes'! Shine your light! Katonda Weebale! Deo Gratias! Thanks be to God!

—*Fr. Christopher LaRocca*

BROTHER ANDREW BIMPEBWA, OCD

My name is Andrew Bimpebwa. I was born in 1980 at Entebbe, the 5th born of 6 children – four boys and two girls. I grew up in Kikonge, a small trading village east of the St Kizito's Church and parish. Since I was active in the parish's youth group, the Xaverians, I got to know the new missionaries from California, and they got to know me! I was privileged to help the priests as a companion in their ministry and translator of their homilies at Mass. These men and lay missionary, Madame Lillian, inspired me to join their community. It took me some time to discern my vocation as a Brother in the Carmelite Order. I studied for a while at the PCJ in Jinja, during which time I stayed at the Comboni Formation house. Their students also attended PCJ. Then in Kenya, I continued my studies at the Tangaza College, Nairobi, which was close to our International Formation center. Fr. Steven Payne, OCD, was another inspiring missionary who guided and helped me.

My next stop was Malawi for my official canonical Novitiate year in 2008-2009, where I made my first profession as a Carmelite. A few years later, on January 3, 2015, I made my final or Solemn Profession, and since then, I have had various assignments at our

Duruelo House in Jinja. Like many other young Ugandan Carmelites, I long for a diverse ministry outside the formation house. In 2016 I received the blessing to come to California and experience the Carmelite way of life in America. It was a great joy to attend the Secular Carmelite Congress in San Jose, accompany Fr. David on his Mission Appeals and promotion journeys to various parishes, and meet the lovely lady, Mary Frazier from Monterey who sponsored my formation as a Carmelite. We have become good friends.

It has been interesting to live with the Muzungu missionaries and formators. Among the many special memories are the community "Happy Hours" for feast days or when visiting Friars came to Jinja, the stress on silence in the community and getting familiar with Carmelite authors of spirituality; also working together in ministry with our American brothers. At the beginning of my time with the Carmelites, there was, for us native Africans, the unusual experience of using tools (knives and forks) at meals in place of what we knew when growing up – the God-given tools - our fingers! Finally, I also gratefully remember our leaders' desire to work with us for a clear vision of our community among the people of our country. We pray that this vision may grow and be blessed by God and by Our Lady of Mount Carmel.

—*Bro. Andrew Bimpebwa*

FR. RICHARD OPENDI, OCD

I am Richard Opendi of the Japadhola tribe – one of the smaller tribes from the Eastern part of Uganda close to the Kenya border.

When I began to seriously think about and pursue my desire to be a priest, I shared my feelings with my uncle, Fr. Valerian Okecho, a diocesan priest. At that time, we were frequently experiencing pockets of insurgence by the Lakwena Movement against the National Resistance Movement (NRM) – the Government of Yoweri Museveni. That disturbance had paralyzed our education system and infrastructure. My uncle, Fr. Valerian, keen to help me, contacted Bishop Joseph Mukwaya of Kiyinda-Mityana, regarding the possibility of joining his diocese. The Bishop accepted me for a probation period of two years and requested that I do the Advanced level of secondary education at the Diocesan Minor Seminary in Mubende.

I spent my vacation period at the Diocesan Administrative residence. I learned about the Carmelite Nuns, whose monastery is adjacent to the Diocesan Cathedral and the Bishop's residence. I frequently went to the monastery to deliver messages about changes of time for the Masses celebrated by the priests from the Diocesan residence. One day, I took the courage to ask the out-sister about what happens inside the monastery. I enquired whether they have men who live like them in Uganda. She told me that the

176

men Carmelites are not in Uganda. They are in Kenya. We got to be good friends; her name was Sr. Ulrike; she has since passed on to her eternal reward.

After my Advanced Secondary School, when I left the Kiyinda-Mityana area, I stayed with my uncle Fr. Valerian Okecho in his new parish of St. Jude at the Busia border near Kenya. I met a seminarian who was in transit back to the seminary of the Apostles of Jesus in Kenya, and I asked him if he knew any of the Carmelites in Kenya. He was happy to tell me that the Carmelite House was close to their house and that some of them were studying at their Apostles of Jesus seminary. Immediately, I decided to apply to the Vocation Director and gave him the letter for delivery by hand.

Soon I got a reply from the Vocations Director, Fr. David Costello, who invited me to visit the Carmelite community in Nairobi. I was delighted with the invitation and did visit the community. Unfortunately, in 1997 I missed that year's intake of postulants because I had not yet processed my travel documents. I joined the Discalced Carmelites formally in Kenya, a mission of the Washington Province of the USA. I lived with an international community of Americans, Australians, Irish, Indians, and Africans from many different parts of the continent.

It is a challenge to live with the Wazungu (the precise plural form of the word muzungu - editor's comment), people I never shared or interacted with before in my life! Meeting them in a mature community of formation makes it more difficult to tell them what I am feeling or going through in life. At the beginning of my time there, I did not tell them about my family. I feared dismissal because I am from a poor family. One day I was asked by my Postulant Master about what type of house I sleep in at home. I described the house as mud bricks and grass-thatched with only one door. I was shocked when he retorted that my father should answer a charge in a court of law as to why he constructed such a house! During vacation time at home, I narrated the story to my dad; he has since passed on. My dad laughed and said, "is that Muzungu normal"? He cautioned me to be careful with those Wazungus. When I had one of my teeth extracted, my dad surmised the cause was the muzungu food. For himself, he claimed that he never had tooth problems to the extent of not having even one removed in his lifetime. This kind of instruction froze my close interaction with the wazungu!

I joined the Carmelites in 1997, made my first profession in 2002, my solemn profession in 2007, and my ordination as a priest in 2008 - praise God! I have been privileged to serve the Order of Carmel in different ministries within the Kenya region and volunteered to minister in my own country for the California- Arizona mission. Unfortunately, I could not minister at St. Kizito, Kyengeza parish, but I did serve in the formation house at Jinja. In all, I have found much enrichment and considerable fulfillment from the experience of living in multicultural communities. No matter where we go, we are challenged to adapt and adjust to new realities and humbly understand why things are said and done.

—Fr. Richard Opendi

BROTHER EMMANUEL MAYINJA, OCD

I am Emmanuel Mayinja, born on December 26th, 1978 (just a day late for Christmas) at Rubaga, Uganda, and grew up in a good Catholic family. My father died recently on November 1st, 2018; God rest his soul. When I was growing up, I used to tell my parents that I would like to be a brother because, in the village, we had a Christian Brother to whom I looked up and who was a great inspiration for me. In 2008 I joined the Carmelite Friars, went to the Novitiate, and made my first profession on the feast of Our Lady of Mount Carmel, July 16th, 2009, and my solemn vows on January 23rd, 2016.

Vocation is a call from God and comes in many voices; as well as the inspiration of the Christian Brother already mentioned, I think living in a good Catholic family was a substantial influence on my decision to become a brother. Now, as a Carmelite friar, I am sustained by the Carmelite way of living and by the charism of interior prayer, which I greatly treasure. Reading the history of the Carmelite saints and seeing their lives in relationship to Sacred Scripture, as well as sharing the everyday life in the community, has helped me to mature as a religious in the Carmelite family. I thank God for the gift of my vocation.

Living with some muzungu friars was a curious experience; it took me some time to adjust to their different accents, their strange pronunciation of words even among themselves. The term "water" seemed to be pronounced differently by each one! That trained us native Ugandans to cultivate a listening ear. After supper, we went to the living room and listened to the news on Fr. David's little radio, which he gave to me before he left Uganda and which I still treasure. As well as the report of world events from the BBC, the recreation time was full of teasing and jokes and consequently never dull.

Sometimes Fr. Paul produced his playing cards and amused us with many tricks; he also entertained the Bishop with the card games when he came to the parish on Pastoral Visitation. Another memory stood out when Fr. David visited us with pilgrims in 2010; we had a Mass at Magonga when the deacon, Brother David Guzman, was presented with a live chicken at the Offertory. He was so delighted and fascinated that he held the chicken like a newborn baby; it was his first time touching an African chicken.

We are grateful for the times Fr. David spent with us at Kyengeza and on Pilgrimage, preparing us for the next stage of our growth and carrying on God's work of evangelization.

—Bro. Emmanuel Mayinja

FR GODFREY CHANDYA LEGA, OCD

I am Fr. Godfrey Chandya Lega. I was born at Bibia in the northeast of Uganda on March 26th, 1977. I joined the Carmelites as an ordained priest and made my profession as a Carmelite on August 22nd at Kyengeza, after my novitiate in Nigeria. The Carmelite charism of interior prayer, a life of allegiance to Jesus Christ, and community life are what attracted me to the Order of Carmel. The lives of the Carmelite saints who left a rich heritage of spirituality for all who desire to follow them and attain to perfect union with God are also a great inspiration. We are sustained in our vocation by constant communion with God through the Eucharist, personal and communal prayer, the Word of God, as well as our own Rule and Constitutions.

Father David congratulates Father Godfrey on
his porfession as a Carmelite

Being an African among the "wazungu" is a challenge; however, my personal experience is that it depends on whether a person is knowledgeable about the Carmelite life or has embraced it. I have been privileged to experience it in Africa and the USA. The Provincial sent me to our parish of Santa Cruz in Arizona, and there our community of four was international – an American, a Mexican, an Irishman, and myself, a Ugandan! It was somehow like living with different people of different tribes in Africa! We are different, but we adjust.

I understand that the wazungu are mentoring us Ugandans to be better Carmelites in the U.S.A. and Africa. We all look forward to when we will be entrusted with more responsibilities so that the seed of Carmel, already planted by the wazungu, can mature and bring forth new Carmelite fruit in Americans and Ugandans for the glory of God.

—*Fr. Godfrey Chandya Lega*

PROSCOVIA NANFUKA

My name is Proscovia Nanfuka, a native Ugandan who worked as a secretary with the Carmelite Friars during their stay at Kyengeza parish in the Kiyinda-Mityana diocese from November 2005 to August 2010. I connected to the Carmelite mission through one of their volunteers – Lillian Kelly. She had visited my uncle, Fr James Kabuye, when he was chaplain at St Kizito Bethany High School.

I am currently working with Caritas, Kiyinda-Mityana Diocese, in the Social protection office dealing with orphans, vulnerable children, and people with disabilities.

I have many memories of working with the Carmelite priests, mainly Fr David, the parish priest at that time. Here are some of these memories.

PICNICS: Every year after Christmas, the priests and the Rectory staff had a day out together - a picnic. That was a completely new experience for me. On December 27th, just a few months after being hired, we went to the hills of Banda, where Fr Josaphat Kasambula, who was working with the Carmelite priests, brought us to his family's land. Being a simple village person, I dressed up in my Sunday's best with high heels, ready to go. I soon realized that a more straightforward dress and shoes were all I needed. I had to play football and netball and the other activities barefooted. At the cost of a few bruised toes, I learned my lesson and never messed up again at the next picnics. Being from a village out in the bush, I did not know any better. Can you believe it; that was my very first picnic! I thank the Carmelite community and staff that they did not make fun of me; if it had been a different group, they would have put a lot of shame on me.

Prossy in her office

POLICE: One time in Kampala, Uganda's capital city, shopping for various items for the mission, we got lost. Trying to get back on track, Fr David chanced to make an illegal U-turn, and immediately an onsite traffic policeman flagged us down, watched by a curious group of onlookers. I realized that we would have to go to the police station for questioning, which would be a long session and undoubtedly end with a good "fine" for the muzungu priest. I told Fr David to move on cautiously as if he were looking for a good parking spot and be ready to negotiate a settlement with the policeman. We finally parked, and the policeman was proper with us; we humbly admitted our mistake in breaking the law and offered 30,00.00 UGX (a little less than 10 dollars at that time) for himself. He gratefully accepted it, and we were free! Praise God!

UNFORGETTABLE: My most grateful memory is how the Carmelites gave me a great gift for life – a University education. I did not have a mother or a father, and they treated me like their very own child. I was never in need as I completed my course for a second-class degree as a Bachelor of Science in Business Economics. That was the practical help of Fr Stephen on the recommendation of Fr David. I am very grateful.

HOSPITAL: Finally, when Fr David was very sick, Judith, one of the kitchen staff, and I stayed with him in the St Francis Hospital at Nsambya. From his sickbed, Fr David whispered to me, "if I die, I want them to bury me with the poor people behind the main hall at Kyengeza." His words hit me hard; I had to go outside and cry, thinking that he was about to pass away. Later, when recovering somewhat, we took him out in his wheelchair to get a change of air. We saw a casket being removed from the hospital and put in a vehicle; he said to us, "look, that is the way you will take me back to Kyengeza." His words shocked and upset me very much, and I began to think of myself trying to explain to the Christians at Kyengeza what happened to him. Happily, I did not have to do that; he recovered somewhat and returned to Kyengeza in a different type of transport.; but we still had to bid him a painful farewell as he left for further treatment in California. I pray for his dear life and thank God that he is still with us and serving God's people, alas not in Kyengeza but Arizona. Fr David, may God bless you.

—*Proscovia Nanfuka*

FATHER PAUL KOENIG, OCD

Fr. Paul Koenig here. When our Provincial, Fr. Gerald Werner, first asked me if I would be willing to serve in our mission in Uganda ("Equatorial East Africa" has such an exotic ring to it, don't you think?), I told him I would be, but that the most challenging part of it would be for me to leave my parents. They were both in their mid-80's and spending time with them got more and more precious as the years rolled along. I have nothing against your folks, but my parents are the "best ever." When I told them that the Provincial asked me if I would be willing to go to Uganda, Dad, God bless him, replied, "Don't let us be a factor in your decision." That helped make this difficult part much more manageable. When I said "Yes" to Fr. Gerald's request, he replied, "I am assigning you to the mission." The first people I told were Mom and Dad – through my tears. This time, it was Mom who spoke first: "Both of us think this is a great opportunity for you." As I told you, they were the "best ever"! As it turned out, when I left for Uganda, that was the last time I would see Dad. He passed away just before I came home for my first vacation back from Africa. Mom passed just fourteen months later. May they both rest in peace.

At the conclusion of his General Visitation of our province in 1999, Fr. Gerry Fitzpatrick announced to us that Fr. General would like our Province to consider the possibility of founding a mission in Africa, that Rome felt that "the time was ripe" for starting a mission in Uganda. The simple fact that Rome was requesting this of us provided all the motivation I needed to be open to the possibility of serving. When asked if I would go in 2007, I was ready and willing.

Years earlier, I had heard it said that two things join people together, transcending whatever differences that might keep them apart: music and sports. I found that to be true when I arrived in Africa. I had anticipated the music in Africa to be simple, primitive. But I discovered it to be so lively, full of complex harmonies, and utterly transporting – so alive! The captivating rhythms course through the veins of the African people. It moves you.

When you talk to an African kid, guaranteed within five minutes, he will ask you: "What football team do you support, Fazah (Father)"? The game to which he is referring is the sport we call soccer, and he is talking about the Premier League, professional soccer from England. So right off the bat, you are connected.

One of my favorite people whom I met over there was a kid. I suppose I should call him a young man. Peter was a student at our secondary school (high school) at our parish of St. Kizito (named after the youngest of the Ugandan Martyrs – he was just 14 when he gave his life for the Faith and whose feast-day we celebrate on June 3rd, "St Charles Lwanga and Companions"). Peter was a great drummer. Not only did he have a good rhythm, but he also played those drums – four at a time, mind you! – with a particular texture. What a touch! He could make those skins talk, I tell you! Speaking of talking, since our Luganda (the local native language) was limited, we would call upon the services of a congregation member to assist us with the task of translating our homilies. Peter was my favorite. He was lively, animated, and always brought a certain endearing sense of humor to his translating. You could see he was popular with his fellow students and appreciated by all the parishioners.

Along with his ever-present smile, Peter's face had another striking characteristic. Seared across his forehead about an inch apart, he had three parallel horizontal scars. At first, I thought they might have been a residual evidence of some tribal initiation rite of some sort. As it turns out, a local revolutionary sect took him captive. He attempted to escape and was shot in the leg as he ran away. When they returned to the camp, they took a hot iron from the fire and branded him with those three scars across his forehead, admonishing him never to try to run away again. Sometime later, he did attempt to get away again, this time making good his escape.

In 2012, I was assigned back to our parish of St. Cecilia in Stanwood, Washington. One morning I saw the latest edition of our mission newsletter had arrived at the parish office. I anxiously scooped it up to get the latest news. There, on the front page, was a photograph of Peter. Wow, I thought, what was up with Peter that he would land with a photo on the front page? I was so excited! As I read on, suddenly I felt as if someone had kicked me in the stomach. Peter was dead! From hepatitis! I was in shock. That could not be happening. How could it be so?

I had hepatitis when I was twenty-one. You go to the doctor, get treatment for it, get better, and carry on, not so in Africa. You get sick and die. It hit me like a ton of bricks. We help a lot of people in Uganda. Simple medical treatments save lives. Just as importantly, we learn from them. It is a great blessing that we have a mission presence in Africa. Thanks be to God.

—*Fr Paul Koenig*

FR COLM STONE'S UPDATE
(after returning from the mission to the USA.)

It is a long way from our Mission in Kyengeza, Uganda, to our Seminary in Mount Angel, Oregon, and it has taken me at least three months to "arrive" I'm not sure if I am all here yet!

The culture shock has been great. Returning to this land of affluence and abundance after living in a land of extreme poverty has taken some getting used to and settling down. I was driving up from California on the 1-5 freeway, all four lanes of the morning commute going into the city are stopped – thousands of cars going nowhere. I felt sorry for the people sitting there in their cars, unable to do anything about it but wait. Then I thought to myself: "if this were Uganda, there would be no freeway, just dirt tracks: and no cars, just thousands of people, and they would all be talking to one another, as they walked along." So much for progress.

I'm grateful to our Provincial, Fr. Gerald Werner, for giving me the time I needed to get acclimatized. And how wonderful it was to see and visit with old friends again. I am now back at the Carmelite Seminary in Mount Angel, Oregon, and ready – more or less - to take up my duties as assistant to Fr. Christopher LaRocca, who is Rector of our community of 14 Carmelite seminarians.

Looking back at my time at our Uganda Mission, there is no way I can say "it's all behind me." It is all very present to me. It's been a wonderful experience and privilege – I'm full of memories. The people, especially the children, the singers, the dancers, the drummers, the places and special events; the people wielding their hoes in their vegetable gardens, from the very elderly to the merest toddlers, the water-carriers, the stick-gatherers (to make fires for cooking) – I could go on and on reliving those memories. They have changed me and caused me to be a different and hopefully a better person. I cannot and would not want to forget them.

I hope that you will not forget either. Your prayers and support mean so much to the other members of our mission team and me; it was a significant boost to our morale that we had your enthusiastic support for our efforts at the mission. Our mission team continues with their service of God's people at Kyengeza parish with its 15 sub-parishes (in my mind's eye, I can still see the way to each of them), and they continue to need your support. No longer there in body, I am still with them in spirit and hope that you are too.

May God reward your kindness and concern for our people in Uganda, and may you and all your loved ones know God's joy and peace in your hearts

—Fr. Colm Stone

11
LAST WORDS

Earlier in this book, I have expressed the reason for our Carmelite presence in Uganda with the summary words of Pope Paul VI to the religious leaders of the traditional Orders of the Church - "Go to Africa and enrich the local Churches there with your own charism." That is undoubtedly in direct line with the Second Vatican Council's Decree on the Church's Missionary Activity. This great Council document, "Ad Gentes Divinitus" of December 7th, 1965, is, in turn, the modern expression of the great commission of Jesus to His apostles, found on the very last words of the Gospel of Matthew, chapter 28, verse 19-20:

> "Go, therefore, and make disciples of all nations, baptizing them in the name of the Father, and of the Son, and of the Holy Spirit, teaching them to observe all that I have commanded you. And behold, I am with you always, until the end of the age."

The commission is being carried out faithfully by the followers of Jesus in every age, sometimes with great success, other times in struggle and weakness, and even in failure. No faithful follower of Christ can shrink from fidelity to that call.

It is truly a privilege to be part of this venture and in any place. In our Carmelite mission to Uganda, Nuns, Friars, Sisters, and Seculars, find in the words of Jesus and the Vatican Council's missionary decree encouragement and inspiration. Recall some of the following phrases from this document towards the end of chapter 2,

"Different forms of religious life should be promoted in the new Churches so that they might manifest different aspects of Christ's mission and the life of the Church, devote themselves to various pastoral works, and prepare their members to exercise them properly ...

The various undertakings aimed at establishing contemplative life are worthy of special mention; some aim at implanting the rich tradition of their Order and retaining the essential elements of the monastic life; others are returning to the simpler forms of early monasticism. All, however, are eagerly seeking a natural adaptation to local conditions. The contemplative life should be restored everywhere because it belongs to the fullness of the Church's presence." (Vatican Council II, The Conciliar and Post Conciliar Documents, Austin. Flannery O.P. General editor)

This concilliar document is the primary theological training for the missionary activity of the Church and calls for ongoing study and application. It spells out the commission of Jesus for our present times. Before setting out for Kenya, I was fortunate to participate in a month-long Maryknoll course of preparation for future missionaries that helped the approximately 35 participants explore the various human, cultural, theological, and spiritual aspects of missionary life. Later, I was disappointed to find a certain unwillingness among our friars to undergo any similar type of preparation. Moving from a first-world affluent society to a country in the developing world is not easy; it can be detrimental to the mission's success to hold on to a uniform view of pastoral work, life, and service in a different culture.

On a practical level, I discovered the writings of Brian Fikkert and the work of his Chalmers Center to be very down-to-earth and helpful. Steve Corbett and Dr. Fikkert authored the best-selling "When Helping Hurts: how to alleviate Poverty without Hurting the poor … and Yourself" and have continued to give practical training through videos and various writings that deal with the reality of poverty in mission lands and the USA. The goal of the work of the Chalmers Center and their reports is to inspire missionaries, NGOs, and donors to foster transformation in the communities they serve and to do this holistically, exploring how to preach the Gospel by word and deed. A recent contribution entitled "Helping without Hurting in Africa" (2021) which includes a Facilitator's Manual by Jonny Kabiswa Kyazze, is typical of their approach. The Chalmers Center is located at 507 McFarland Rd. Suite B., Lookout Mountain, GA 30750 (telephone 706-956-4119).

The need to prepare missionaries and volunteers does not deny the generosity of those who go with curiosity and goodwill. They often claim they have changed – even for life – by the experience. The Spirit of God is always at work and breathes wherever He will. Yet the human preparation cannot be discarded and can only help open the horizons of missionary service to new possibilities.

On a more spiritual level, I was surprised and delighted to be able to avail of the religious helps for growth that I found in Uganda. The native lay community of men and women of the Foyer de Charite (originally from France) near the National Shrine of Namugongo provides an ideal setting for Days of Recollection and retreats from which I and many others enjoyed and benefitted. Likewise, the Comboni retreat house in Namugongo and another on the Masaka Road surprised me with excellent Directed Retreats, conducted by competent retreat masters from the Missionary of Africa and the St Patrick's, Kiltegan communities. I wondered why similar facilities and opportunities seemed to be rarer in California! Maybe my need for spiritual nourishment was heightened by being on mission? Or perhaps it was the simple goodness and appreciation of a grateful people - nuns, priests, sisters, and ordinary lay people - who Bishop Mukwaya reminded me of when he told me how impressed the people are when they see the missionaries praying their Rosary. I experienced this in many ways and recall when I pulled in at a gas station to fill my truck with petrol. I was sent on my way by the young attendant with the words "Thank you, and thank you for being a priest"!

GRATITUDE

We limited human beings cannot give adequate thanks to God for all His infinite goodness and care for us. Fortunately, we have His Beloved Son, our Savior Jesus Christ, whose life work gives adoration, reparation, thanksgiving, and intercession on our behalf and is fully pleasing to God. We touch this especially in the Holy Sacrifice of the Mass.

But it is also essential that I give thanks to all who were human instruments of God's goodness on life's journey. Recalling the years of my African ministry, I know that the foundation for those years came from a good family home in Ireland and my Carmelite family. I can never forget the missionaries who served with me, Carmelite and Diocesan priests, Sisters of Mary of Carmel, and volunteers. Nor can I forget the Provincial leaders of our Calif-Az Province who supported us with annual visits and unfailing encouragement - Fr Stephen Watson, the Founding Provincial who also served generously at Jinja for two years, Fr Gerald Werner, Fr Matthew Williams, and our current leader, Fr Adam Gonzales. They represent the commitment of our Province and always sought out what was best for the Province and the mission. I pray that the Lord Jesus will continue to guide our present mission Superior, Fr Phillip Sullivan, and that other friars will hear and heed the call to serve the people of Uganda in the coming years.

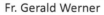
Fr. Gerald Werner   Fr. Adam Gonzales

The local Bishops in Uganda, Bishop Mukwaya and Bishop Zziwa, both from the Kiyinda-Mityana diocese, were always supportive and appreciative. Bishop Willigers of Jinja was a real benefactor to us. Our own Carmelite Nuns and Sisters were a loving presence and a constant joy by their friendship and goodness. The

Diocesan priests treated us with kindness, great respect, and a welcoming spirit. We remember especially those who served with us in Kyengeza and our friends among the Capuchins, the White Fathers, and the Bannakaroli Brothers.

The ordinary people of the mission, "the Christians," brought great joy to our hearts by their welcome, faith, love for God and one another. Our friends and helpers in California and the US, Ireland, and England were outstanding financial supporters. Among them, our Carmelite Nuns and Secular Carmelites can take pride of place in building up the mission.

Let me also add a word of thanks to those who shared their own experiences in chapters 9 and 10. Their personal stories are a significant part of our African Memories. I cannot forget those who helped from our Mission Office in California and the generous assistance from our Santa Cruz parish experts, Hada Reyes and Karen Estavillo. They helped me so many times on the computer and the printer. A special "Thank you" also goes to my editor in Ireland, Therese Grisewood-Quinn, and her husband Frank, whose practical input, patience, and perseverance kept me on track to bring this venture to print. My appreciation also goes to the Wheatmark Publishing Company, especially to Mark Dupaul, the publishing consultant, and Lori Conser, the project manager, for their helpfulness and competence.

Most of the photos in this book were not professionally taken. Many of them are already published in the Mission Newsletters. I am very grateful to our amateur photographers and I send special thanks to the Sisters of Mary of Mount Carmel for the use of the cover photo which is from their archives in their mother house at Linz in Austria.

Therese and Frank Grisewood-Quinn

TITLE WORDS

Finally, I return to the title of these African memories, "Come back tomorrow." Those words spoken by the Post Office assistant in Mityana in the early days of my time in Uganda gave me a jolt as to where I was, some amusement and the thought of writing about the Mission. They remain in my memory, but it was only later in life that they returned in different forms never considered when I first heard them. When I could no longer return to the mission and was given the task as Mission Zelator in California, I subconsciously wanted to return to the place I loved so much. For this, I organized "Mission Pilgrimages," which helped the mission, fulfilled my deepest longings, and were visits of great joy.

Fr. Phillip with a handicapped child

And now, ten years after having to leave the parish of St Kizito, Kyengeza, there is a possibility of returning. We have a small property there, and we own the Little Flower school. Fr Phillip has spoken about a possible return, and the Bishop is open to this reality. How it will develop is undoubtedly in the hands of God and His loving Providence. We need another foundation besides our Formation house in Jinja, and many avenues are possible. A return to Kyengeza would be a further stage of those "prophetic" words of a humble assistant of the Mityana Post Office, as well as a further assurance of God's "stamp" on our missionary venture..

I often pray in the words of the Breviary (Volume III), the antiphon for Evening Prayer (Tuesday, Week II) for the Canticle of Mary, and invite you to join with me.

"Do great things for us, O Lord, for you are Mighty, and Holy is your name."

Appendix

Maps of Ireland and African Nations

IRELAND

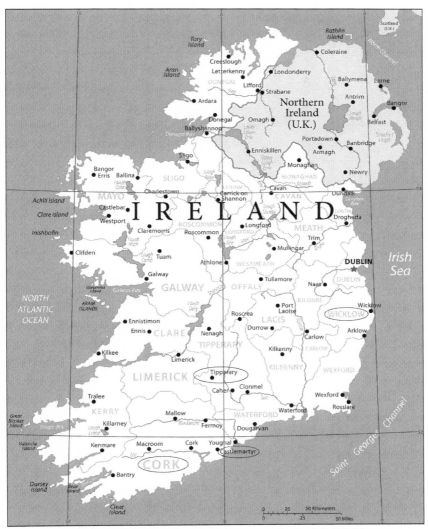

Note locations of Tipperary, Castlemartyr, Co Cork & Wicklow.
Castlemartyr village is located east of Cork city.

AFRICA

Note location of Kenya, Uganda, and Malawi

KENYA

Note location of Nairobi.

UGANDA

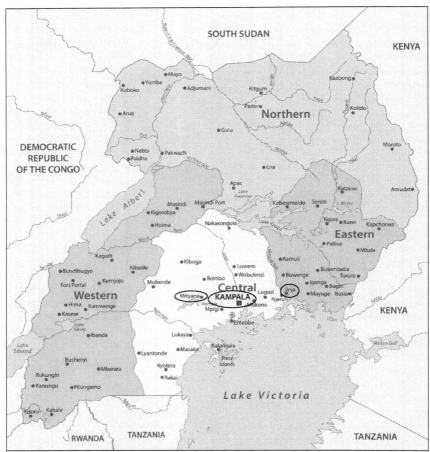

Note locations of Mityana, Kampala, and Jinja – above Lake Victoria.

EAST AFRICAN NATIONS

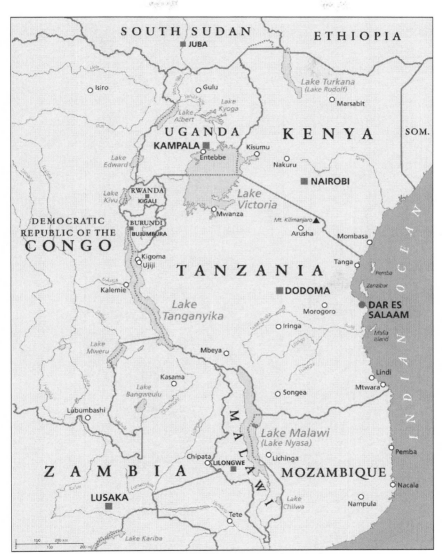

Note locations of Uganda, Kenya, and Malawi below Tanzania

Made in the USA
Las Vegas, NV
24 May 2022